VERMONT AIR

VERMONT AIR

Best of the

VERMONT PUBLIC RADIO

Commentaries

FOREWORD BY MARK VOGELZANG

INTRODUCTION BY BETTY SMITH

EDITED BY PHILIP BARUTH & JOE CITRO

University Press of New England ✍ Hanover and London

University Press of New England, Hanover, NH 03755
This Collection © 2002 Philip Baruth and Joseph A. Citro
Foreword and Introduction © 2002 by University Press of New England
All rights reserved
Printed in Canada
5 4 3 2 1

LIBRARY OF CONGRESS CATALOGING-IN-PUBLICATION DATA

Vermont air : best of the Vermont Public Radio commentaries / foreword by Mark Vogelzang ; introduction by Betty Smith ; edited by Philip Baruth & Joe Citro.

p. cm.

ISBN 1-58465-176-8 (pbk. : alk. paper)

1. New England—Civilization—20th century. 2. New England—Social conditions—20th century. 3. New England—Politics and government—20th century. 4. Vermont—Civilization—20th century. 5. Vermont—Social conditions—20th century. 6. Vermont—Politics and government—20th century. I. Baruth, Philip E. (Philip Edward) II. Citro, Joseph A. III. Vermont Public Radio.

F4.5. V47 2002

814'. 540803274—dc21   2001008178

With great affection and gratitude,

we dedicate this book to Betty Smith,

whose vision, kindness, and artistry have made fans

of those who create these essays for the air.

Contents

Foreword by Mark Vogelzang xiii

Introduction by Betty Smith xv

PHILIP BARUTH
The Great Rondini 1
Which Way the Wind Blows 3
Border Crossing, Hanover, N.H. 6

NICK BOKE
Smoking 9
Confessions of a Vote Counter 12
Lessons from the Hurricane 14

ALLEN BOYE
The Victory Branch 17
The View from the Devil's Hill 19
Submit Adams 21

JOE CITRO
The New England Fat Men's Club 24
That Mystery Girl 26
Spite Cemetery 28

WILL CURTIS
Grandfather's Birthday 31
Christmas 33

Maple Sugaring Time   35

PEG DEVLYN

Prozac for Children?   37

Vermont Job Gap   39

Big Box Schools   42

LOIS EBY

A Passion for Art   44

The Artists at "Out and About"   46

The National Civil Rights Museum   48

ELLEN DAVID FRIEDMAN

Take Back Vermont   50

Globalization   52

The Assignment   54

ALLEN GILBERT

Connecting with Kids   56

Profiles in Courage   58

The First 100   60

VERN GRUBINGER

The Future   63

Kindergarten Worm Visit   65

Mud Season   67

CHERYL HANNA

A Matter of Time   70

Black Ice and White Knights: Vermont's
Good Samaritan Law   72

The Endangered Species Act Doesn't Matter   74

RON KRUPP

Route 30   76

Fanny's Kitchen Garden   78

The Confessions of a Frustrated Gardener   79

WILLEM LANGE

New England Reeling   82

Cato Passes   85

Norm, You're Ruining My Life!   87

TED LEVIN

Of Birds and Baseball   89

Biodiversity and Property Rights   92

A Case Against Catamounts   94

JOHN McCLAUGHRY

Sharp Practice   97

The Rise of the Nanny State   99

Vermont's Coming Crony Capitalism   101

JOHN MORTON

The Torch   104

The Joys of Roller Skiing   106

Competitive Gardening   108

JULES OLDER

Sexual Madness   111

Appropriation   114

Advice to My Daughters on Leaving for College   115

RUTH PAGE

Cockroach 118

Rock Forest 120

Odorwork 123

RON POWERS

Kids and Enchantment 126

Women's Fashions 128

The Youth Problem 130

OLIN ROBISON

The Tenth Anniversary of the Fall of the Wall 132

Turkey 135

Getting Better Results from Our Education System 137

DAN ROCKMORE

A Slice of Pi 141

Getting Lost to Be Found 144

A Geometry of Life 146

MARY BARROSSE SCHWARTZ

The Purple Door 148

Urban Myths and Internet Headaches 149

Child Care Counts 151

BILL SEAMANS

Lexicon 154

Hussein 156

Foreign Legion 158

TOM SLAYTON
Matthiessen 161
Clarinet Man 163
Peacham Tragedy 165

LIBBY STERNBERG
Thank God for the Atom Bomb? 168
Silence Is Not Golden 170
No Excuses! 172

JEFF WENNBERG
The New Counterculture 175
Gillyisms 177
Campaign 2000 Parallels with 1980 179

Afterword by Philip Baruth and Joe Citro 183

Foreword

This collection from Vermont Public Radio's commentary series represents a delightful cross-section of friends whom we know mostly from the sound of their voice and what they like to talk about on the radio. But here, inside this book, you can find some of their best work as words in print.

VPR is the place where these words come to life—where they have the power to sway opinions, or take us to an undiscovered corner of our natural life. It is where stories make us chuckle, or nod our heads in agreement, or make us feel terrific because someone else was able to verbalize how we felt about a particular social or economic issue.

Radio is a ubiquitous and powerful medium, and public radio occupies a unique place in the spectrum of signals, formats, and call letters that make up the radio dial. For many, VPR is a place that feels like home—with voices and personalities that fit like a well-worn pair of slippers, and the kind of music and information and entertainment that makes us feel like we can be a better people.

So it is with great pleasure, as we celebrate VPR's first 25 years, that we share this collection of our commentary friends with you, our listening friends.

Mark Vogelzang
President and General Manager

Introduction

Betty Smith

The story of the VPR Commentary Series is one of shoestrings and innovation. Before VPR signed on the air in August of 1977, there was a lot of discussion over how best to describe our mission. Founding Station Manager Ray Dilley came up with my favorite image. He said that we should simply aim to reflect our audience back to itself.

Simple, right?

Sure.

Deceptively simple.

Devilishly simple.

Because doing this assumes that you know the community you intend to serve. If you don't, you have to get to know it; and then you have to keep current with it over time.

Everything counts: politics, issues, public services, history, traditions, the arts, demographics, you name it. So you learn. You study and investigate.

You try to catch the buzz. What's the topic du jour at the water cooler, the market, the diner and the school? What are we talking about and why? And what does it mean?

But you can't be everywhere at once and you can't become an expert on everything. So you engage. You invite participation. You look for thoughtful people and you listen to them.

You look for the best ideas, the smartest solutions, the most informed opinions, but the community is diverse, so the ideas are diverse. And if you are going to be true to your original objective and reflect the community back to itself honestly, you come to honor diversity. And you trust the community to eventually sort things out for itself through the process of public discourse, to which you contribute through your programming.

As a reporter, you don't surrender your own judgment or values, but you respectfully consider ideas that amplify, and even challenge, your own. In reporting, you try to transcend personal opinion in order to see beyond what you already know.

In commentary, you share what you already know or believe; and you dare to take the considerable risk of sharing your personal opinion as well, as long as it's informed opinion.

In 1988, we wanted to increase our news and information efforts. We also wanted to find a style of presentation that would not duplicate the various services that were already available in the region. We had enjoyed some success with mini-series, having developed "The Nature of Things" with Will Curtis and assisted the National Gardening Association with Ruth Page and "The Gardening Journal." We couldn't yet afford a full-fledged news department—that's the shoestring part. So we decided to experiment with commentary—that's the innovation part. The result was a model that presents voices of the regional community in a narrative and abbreviated format designed specifically for public radio drive time.

We explore the resources, culture, history, and politics of our region through carefully crafted narrative essays written to be spoken aloud. Our commentaries differ from and complement the extemporaneous, excerpted speech of the interview, news story, and arts or lifestyle feature.

The series concept is remarkably flexible. It can and does embrace such diverse elements as informed opinion, public service information, and even humor. It seeks to both entertain and engage the listener. It presents controversial points of view with the confidence that our audience is intelligent and stimulated by ideas and vigorous public discourse.

The scope and depth of the series are determined by the regional community from which it is drawn, a region particularly blessed with thoughtful and articulate people, as well as gifted writers. The potential for variety and diversity is unlimited.

Seen in a time continuum, the series somewhat resembles a vast New England Town Meeting: fairly orderly, sometimes contentious, and often amusing. It is a forum where neighbors meet. The people are real. They live down the road, and they have the courage and generosity to offer their views, talent, and expertise.

The commentary series taps the creative wealth of the regional community in a unique way. While we may suggest topics, and certainly provide editorial guidance and oversight, commentators bring their own fresh ideas to the table. They inform, enrich, and enhance our sense of community. They add a distinctive sense of place, and their voices contribute to VPR's distinctive style and sound.

Our first commentator was Janet Greene. For nearly two years she was the only commentator and was heard on a week-daily basis. In 1988 and 1989 she wrote more than 500 essays on many diverse subjects. She was an obliging and enthusiastic guinea pig for our early ideas about how to craft a short essay series, how to work effectively with writers, and how to write for the ear instead of the eye.

In 1989, Janet's health forced her to cut back to once a week, and other writers were recruited, including Tim Brookes, Rod Clarke, Tom Slayton, Ron Rood, and Olin Robison. In 1990 Ruth Page, Maggie Cassidy, and Bill Eddy joined the group. Madeleine Kunin wrote a series of commentaries beginning in 1991. Joe Citro began his commentaries in 1992, and in 1993 Jane Beck, Bill Seamans, John McClaughry, and Richard Narkewicz joined the series.

In 1994 Nick Boke, Guy MacMillen, Willem Lange, John Morton, and Horace Beck began writing commentaries. In 1995 and 1996 we heard from Jeanne Ryer, Jules Older, Annie Downey, and Mac Parker.

The year 1997 was a very busy one. New voices included Sara Gear, Alison Freeland, Alia Stavrand-Woolf, Susan Sweetser, Peg Devlyn, Girt Lepine, Jenny Nelson, Clark Hinsdale, Libby Sternberg, Ron Powers, Vern Grubinger, Alan Boye, and Ted Levin.

In 1998 we heard from Heidi Pfau, Mary Barrosse, Lois Eby, Dan Rockmore, Philip Baruth, Ron Krupp, and Peter Goldsmith. Also that year, Steve Delaney began his association with VPR as a commentator and Will Curtis made the transition from "The Nature of Things" to the commentary series.

In 1999, the new commentators included Cheryl Hanna, Chester Liebs, Rebecca Coffey, Alex Aldrich, Alexis Jetter, Michael Roche, and Dwight Curry. Since then we have added Ellen David Friedman, David Clarkson, Beth Schmidt, Charles Johnson,

Edith Hunter, Frank Bryan, Jeff Wennberg, Charlie Nardozzi, and David Moats.

That's a list of more than sixty names, and the topics covered have been so numerous, I can't even begin to enumerate them. If you figure a minimum of two commentaries every weekday for thirteen years, the total number of commentaries comes to well over six thousand. (And by the way, I combed the files in an effort to get the dates right and include everyone, but if I have a year wrong or have left anyone out . . . please forgive. Thirteen years of files is a lot of files! And if some names are less familiar, it may be that the person contributed just one commentary to an Impact Series, or that he or she is no longer active, but as with pledges . . . every one counts.)

For the first eight years, we concentrated mainly on feature commentaries, but in 1997, as our News Department grew, we made a concerted effort to add news and issue commentaries. In 1999 we revised our air schedule in order to divide the series into two "groups," one for news and one for feature material.

In 1996, commentaries were included in VPR's first Impact Series, and they have provided additional variety and depth to those efforts ever since.

The series was recently recognized by the Vermont Associated Press Broadcasters Association, with the award for best radio and television commentary in 2000. We submitted a list of eight commentaries as a representative sample of a large group of very diverse opinions on the civil union debate. Additional commentaries were of equal merit on the subject, but the awards were limited to calendar year 2000. The judges were especially impressed by the variety of perspectives. The eight included John McClaughry on the Supreme Court, Peg Devlyn on equal rights, Allen Gilbert on civil versus sacred, Jules Older on the threat to traditional marriage, Libby Sternberg on the constitutional amendment process, Alexis Jetter on Jim Crow laws, Libby Sternberg again on the comparison with race-based civil rights, and Allen Gilbert again on the risk taken by legislators.

From the beginning, we have pursued an overall sense of "balance" in the series, but the process is complicated and our writers are encouraged to write at whatever frequency best fits their lives and as subjects assert themselves. This tends to give us variety as well as the strongest and most timely content.

Gender, age, political point of view, geography, and issue expertise are among the many characteristics that we consider as the series unfolds.

And unfold it will. To me, the most exciting characteristic of the commentary series is that it is open-ended, ever-changing, and, given the nature of radio—which is air after all—you always need new material for tomorrow.

VERMONT AIR

Philip Baruth teaches in the English Department at the University of Vermont. He is the author of three novels, The Millennium Shows *(Albion, 1994),* The Dream of the White Village *(Onion River Press, 1999), and* The X–President *(Bantam Books, 2003). In addition to his commentaries, Philip hosts* Camel's Hump Radio, *a half-hour program on Vermont Public Radio featuring excerpts from classic adventure stories for young readers.*

Called "Notes from the New Vermont," Philip's commentaries often focus on the state's urban centers, and the problems and paradoxes of urban life. A subset of these commentaries makes use of an ironic alias known as the Urban Troubleshooter. Inexplicably, the Urban Troubleshooter is locked in an ongoing power struggle with Vermont Public Radio's otherwise mild-mannered weather forecasters, Steve Maleski and Mark Breen.
(AUTHOR PHOTO BY ANNIKA LJUNG-BARUTH.)

THE GREAT RONDINI

A CITY ISN'T A CITY without street theater, in Vermont or anywhere else. Because it's street theater that renders the urban human, and humane.

Until last year, the best street theater I'd ever seen was on the boardwalk in Venice Beach, California. Venice Beach is what the whole world will be like when Southern California secedes and defeats NATO in World War III: equal parts freak show, fashion show, and prison weight-lifting facility. There were jugglers and accordion players, but the best was a tiny little mime, a Rumanian guy about five foot one. He'd offer a little girl a kite that wasn't really there, and he'd do it so painstakingly that she'd actually reach for it.

During the show I saw, he turned and accidentally ran smack into a group of five really psychopathic-looking weight lifters. The biggest one swore at him and shoved him so hard that he fell off the boardwalk and down into the sand.

Then the little mime got up and you could see a century of Rumanian anger build up in his face, and he flashed his middle finger at the bodybuilders and held it there. No one made a sound. Then they rushed him and grabbed him, and before anyone could move, they began to punch and kick him—all in beautifully slow motion.

Finally, they started bearing him out to sea, like a corpse, and the audience came out of its trance and went wild, and it was all part of the show. Like I say, it was the best I'd ever seen until last year, when I caught the Great Rondini down on the Church Street Marketplace in Burlington.

Rondini is an extremely powerfully built black man somewhere in his mid forties, with an accent that might be Miami by way of the Caribbean. He stands about five eight and wears a sheer black sash over a shaved head, but what makes him the Great Rondini is that he's a magician and an escape artist. He sets up a blanket in front of Leunig's Bistro, nearly every weekend night, and he performs for big crowds every hour on the hour.

Rondini's not the world's greatest magician; you can see him palm-drop a card or a coin without too much trouble. And his patter is workmanlike. He goes through it diligently, good-naturedly, the same jokes at the same moments in the show, putting the crowd in the mood for the finale. Because that's when he shines, that's when Rondini becomes truly Great, when he picks two husky guys out of the audience and directs them to chain him up and padlock him as tightly as they can. "Do not be afraid to draw the chains tight," he tells the two men. "Pull harder, tighter."

The best way to tell it to you is to describe what you see when you swing around the corner of Pearl Street onto the Marketplace. It's mid August and you're angling down toward lower Church because you're thinking about some Szechuan broccoli, and you see a huge ring of people in front of Leunig's, a crowd so big it jams the entire street. And these people aren't just passing time, they're *fascinated*, pushing in toward the center and sticking their faces over one another's shoulders.

Finally you push inside the circle: You see two large white men with a massive black man held between them, bound in locks and chains, standing on a small block in the absolute heart of the Marketplace. It's symbolism so vast and so deep that no one sees it, no one acknowledges it, but everyone feels it like a car alarm going off at the very edge of their consciousness.

Sometimes, though not always, Rondini's is the only black face on the entire street as he stands there, the center of a phantom auction. It's exactly like when the tiny mime in Venice Beach insulted the body builders: Nobody moves, nobody really breathes.

And then Rondini tells the audience, "Please feel free to shout encouragement," and people do. He lets it build and then starts to shiver a little, as though he's testing the chains. Then he brings his right shoulder down hard, and you see it do what a shoulder shouldn't do, pop out and forward, and a bight of the chain swings free.

People really start to lose it then, yelling and whistling, and next Rondini's down on his knees and he's shimmying and loops of chain drop away like dead skin. The applause gets louder, and he works harder.

And after bringing you back two hundred and fifty years and locking himself securely into an image all Americans have stored away deep in their communal memory, Rondini escapes. And he brings every man, woman, and child in that audience out with him, every time.

WHICH WAY THE WIND BLOWS

(Urban Troubleshooter Series)

✦

EVEN THE BEST URBAN troubleshooter knows the green-potato-chip taste of failure. Case in point: When Batman first met the Joker, he thought he was going up against some punk in clown makeup, and then—Whammo!—he had an arch nemesis. That always makes me feel better, because that's exactly how it was when I first tangled with Steve Maleski, VPR's Eye-on-the-Sky Weather Forecaster.

It seemed routine enough at first: My contact met me at a contra dance in West Addison. Between sets, he wiped his forehead and whispered to me. "It's the Fairbanks Museum in St. Johnsbury. We've been monitoring Maleski's forecasts. He's gone from 93% to 100% correct."

"So he's good," I said, "we knew that all along."

"Look," he hissed, "100% success isn't weather forecasting— it's weather *making*. Yesterday we located an unidentified satellite in geosynchronous orbit. Maleski's been using it to control the weather. He's manipulating the primaries in New Hampshire— east of the Green Mountains—by sleeting on selected candidate events. He may be almost entirely responsible for Al Gore."

Just then his partner grabbed my contact's hand, and he whirled away. I didn't need a weatherman to know which way the wind blew.

Just outside St. Johnsbury, a turbulent air mass aloft forced my car into a spin. Maleski's work, no doubt. Two stone lions guarded the front of the Fairbanks Museum, and as I walked between them needles of sleet stabbed at my neck.

The door to the museum was open. I hit the lights, and my heart stopped. Below stained glass windows and an arched wood ceiling were huge diorama cases filled with animals from all over the world: a polar bear pawing a downed seal, flamingoes and dinosaurs and snarling marsupials and a flock of stuffed birds of all colors. It was like walking into Noah's Ark during a storm at sea, and finding the animals frozen by some unseen Hand. I got the message: *Mess with me*, Maleski was saying, *and I'll make the Great Flood look like scattered precipitation.*

The Weather Center was in the sub-sub-basement. Computer weather models glowed neon green and purple and yellow, tracking wind and storm everywhere in the world. One wall was a huge Lucite situation map like the Pentagon uses, and standing before it was a trim, mild-mannered man with a neat black beard and ponytail. "Come in, troubleshooter," he said softly. "I'm sure it's cold outside."

I stayed where I was. "I'm sure you know *exactly* how cold it is," I snapped.

Maleski chuckled. "Of course. Five degrees Fahrenheit, which is—"

"Minus fifteen Celsius," I cut in smoothly.

He turned slowly. "You're good, troubleshooter. But not good enough. You come here thinking I'll reveal my master plan and then you'll overpower me and stop it. You've been watching too many 007 movies."

He was right. I'd been thinking of *Goldfinger* the whole time.

"I'll tell you the plan but it will do you no good. Yes, I have a secret weather-making satellite. Man has warped the natural weather patterns. Politicians promise action, then do nothing. Look at Al Gore."

He gave a sardonic laugh. "They don't realize the pain that a midlevel disturbance causes me. So I have taken it upon myself to undo the effects of global warming. And yes, part of the plan is to make sure only pro-environmental candidates succeed in New Hampshire."

"You'll never get away with this," I said through clenched teeth.

"Fortunately for the world, that isn't so. Good-bye, troubleshooter." Maleski smiled, and someone struck me from behind. I'd forgotten about Mark Breen.

When I came to, I was in a booth at the Hilltopper Lounge in downtown St. Johnsbury. A waitress there named Loretta was prepared to swear that I'd had one too many and passed out. Maleski had thought of everything.

In fact, when I went to call my people, I found he'd given me some sort of posthypnotic suggestion, preventing me from saying a word. The only way around it is to use voice-over narration, the way I'm doing now.

So that's the story. The world's weather is returning slowly to normal, which I should be grateful for, but it's hard. Batman had the Joker, and I've got Steve Maleski, and I have to live with that every day of my life. And living with losing has a way of making even the most brilliant day seem variably cloudy.

BORDER CROSSING, HANOVER, N.H.

(The Good, The Bad, & The Sushi)

❧

IT IS WEDNESDAY, eleven o'clock in the morning, and I'm headed south to the new interstate border crossing at Hanover, New Hampshire. On the New Hampshire side, two friends are waiting for me at an out-of-the-way sushi bar. This trip used to be a snap. But after watching a ten-year wave of progressive legislation surge out of the Vermont Legislature, including the use of property taxes to equalize school funding, New Hampshire just went ahead and sealed the border with Vermont down tight, airtight, like a Ziploc freezer bag.

Now you have to be cleared through a checkpoint to enter. Granted, eventually you learn how to avoid being separated from the herd and searched. But it's not fun.

When I reach the Ledyard bridge, I'm stunned by it, as always. It's a knock-out bit of architectural whimsy, spanning a sweet stretch of the Connecticut river. The design is a wild cross between ancient Egypt and Toys 'R Us: bright green railings set off massive granite blocks, and all of this is topped by twelve stupendous balls of concrete, some of them eight or nine feet high.

Six of these big balls sit on either side of the bridge, and you'd expect that Vermont would have claimed six balls and New Hampshire six, like two old women breaking a carton of eggs in half at the corner market.

But not so. New Hampshire wound up with all the balls.

The border crossing sits just at the foot of the dense pines protecting Hanover. Today it's only a ten-minute wait before the guard motions me to the booth. He's a tall man, lean, not much flab on him. All of the New Hampshire Interstate border guards look like this guy, which I can only guess comes from years of living free and not dying. "State of residence," he says flatly.

"Vermont," I answer quietly. You can't be too subservient or you'll arouse contempt; still, you don't want to seem cocky. He's wearing wrap-around sunglasses but without being asked I take mine off, so he can evaluate my eyes.

"Purpose of your visit to New Hampshire?"

"Meeting friends in Hanover for sushi."

His eyebrows twitch, nothing heavy, but clearly we've left routine territory. He pulls a little notebook out of his breast pocket, scans it.

"You know it's illegal to bring wasabi mustard back across state lines."

I tell him I do.

"Will you be eating just sushi, or sashimi as well?"

This is one of those questions you never know how to answer, because you're not quite sure what they're after, but I figure the truth will set you free, so I say, "Probably a little of both. Sushi and sashimi."

"*Both*," he repeats, and he straightens visibly in his seat. I sense intense interest now. Clearly I've just finished fleshing out one of their current profiles. I do my best to look like a harmless daytripper. Just another good-timin', sashimi-eatin', chuckle-headed Vermonter headed into the Granite State for a little R&R.

And then he hits me with the heavy artillery. "While in the Granite State do you plan to militate for and/or disseminate political literature favoring a state income tax, sales tax, or other unwarranted levy on taxpayers or owners of real property?"

I can tell that this is it, this question is the invisible fork in the road. If I answer correctly, I will be allowed to pass and in ten minutes I'll be laughing about this in the Panda's sunken dining room.

If I answer incorrectly I will be taking the road less traveled, and it will make all the difference: My car will be dissected, and when they find no pro-tax literature bagged in the gas tank, they will turn their attentions to me.

So I think hard, and I get it right. "No sir," I say. "In fact, after lunch I have an appointment with a real estate agent to look at property on this side of the river."

For a second I think I've overdone it, but then he gives me a grudging smile. "You wouldn't be the first, son," he says, and he's just about to move me on, when he spies a copy of *The New York Times* sticking out from under the back seat.

And that's all she wrote.

He gives me this look like, *nice try*, and he waves me over to the side of the road, where four other guards are waiting.

"We'd like to have a quick look in your trunk, sir, if you don't mind," the border guard says smoothly, but that's not what I hear. What I hear is, [Voice from *Treasure of the Sierra Madres*] "Badges? We don't need no stinking badges."

This is Philip Baruth, and this was satire. Please don't call my house.

Nick Boke is a free-lance writer who, if he had his druthers, would spend all his time writing commentary for VPR. Instead, he also works for organizations such as the Vermont Center for the Book, the Vermont Reads Institute, and others, helping make books and reading and ideas and conversation part of everybody's everyday life. Come Sunday, he's in the pulpit at the First Universalist Parish of Chester. (AUTHOR PHOTO BY BUFFY BOKE.)

SMOKING

UNTIL JOCELYN ELDERS came out with her controversial comments about the relationship between illegal drugs and violence, I'd resolved not to take up one of my VPR blocks with some sort of "confessions of a nicotine addict."

There're lots of reasons not to write about what it's like to quit smoking cigarettes. The first is that in writing about this subject I'm admitting publicly that for twenty-five years a little white tube of vegetable matter lay at the center of my life.

If I had a pack of cigarettes in my pocket, life was good. If I didn't, it wasn't. Making admissions like this is pretty embarrassing.

An even more compelling reason for not going public with my years as a smoker and my months as a nonsmoker is that, by and large, it's a pretty boring subject. There's a big part of me that wants to say, "Enough! Just forget about it! It was dumb, but you've quit. Get on with your life. Quit thinking about smoking."

But you see, that's the point.

Those who have recently stopped smoking can't just get on with their lives. They have to work very hard at systematically *Not Smoking*. This takes time and energy, concentration, and willpower.

I've been told it gets easier. Eventually, I hear, I won't periodically break out in tears for no apparent reason, or have to reexplain to myself in great detail why it would not be a good idea to take up smoking again.

Right now, it's harder to get up in the morning than it used to be. It's harder to write, to concentrate, to talk, to . . . well, just about everything.

Several years ago, I began to compare the impact of my addiction to nicotine on my life with the impact of heroin on the lives of those addicted to that drug.

There were some big differences. For example, as a nicotine addict, all I had to do when I ran out of my drug was to go to the store and buy more. And I could support my habit for a little over a dollar a day if I stuck with the generic brands.

So I might get a little shaky every now and then, but I could always count on being able to get hold of what I needed.

But if the drug I'd experimented with twenty-five years ago had been one of the illegal ones instead of one of the legal ones, imagine the impact the addiction would have had on me.

Rather than wondering if I should pick up a quart of milk when I bought my fix, I'd have had to keep tabs on the underground world of dealers and the arcane world of drug shipments.

If I'd dropped by to get my fix and found the dealer didn't have any, I wouldn't just have driven on to the next convenience store. I'd have hung out with the dealer, waiting, shaking as badly as a nicotine addict who hasn't smoked for an hour or two, thinking about nothing but my next hit. I'd have missed meetings, skipped phone calls. I sure wouldn't have gotten around to writing any VPR commentaries.

And my drug, being illegal, would have cost me a hell of a lot more than a dollar a day. The high price of illegal drugs is one of those rare situations where market economic theory clearly works—the price is so high because my dealer is charging me for the high risks he runs.

So there I'd have been, heading out of the economic and social loop because society had said the addiction I'd chosen was not an acceptable one.

As I contemplated the connections between me the cigarette

smoker and the heroin addict, I began to take a new look at society's intensifying attacks on nicotine addiction.

Where we could smoke was being curtailed. Higher sin taxes seemed a pretty good way to pay for the coming health-care program. It would only be logical to deny smokers certain medical treatments, since they had dug their own graves.

It was obviously becoming more uncomfortable, impractical, and expensive to smoke cigarettes. Would it also become illegal?

If it became illegal, a network of nicotine dealers would spring up on our backroads and in our alleyways. I knew I'd find them, pay their price, take their risks, dodging the violence that would accompany the staking out of their territories. I would become part of all that.

In August I quit smoking.

In December I'm beginning to pick up the pieces.

But I've been thinking a lot about the horrible injustice we've created with our drug policies.

Nicotine addicts safely purchase reasonably priced fixes almost anywhere. Those addicted to illegal drugs—simply because our society has decided that these addictions are not acceptable—are forced out of society into marginalized lives of poverty, crime, shame, and violence.

Am I saying that more drugs should be legalized or that legal ones should be criminalized?

No. I'm merely pointing out one of our society's greatest injustices. Maybe if we looked at the drug problem in this light rather than in a good-versus-evil light we might get somewhere.

I can certainly say that from the standpoint of the history of the addiction of this middle-aged American male, Jocelyn Elders' remarks deserve a lot more serious consideration than the political establishment has thus far given them.

CONFESSIONS OF A VOTE COUNTER

IT WAS A LITTLE BEFORE seven P.M. when I showed up at Martin Memorial Hall in Weathersfield on Tuesday, first to vote, then to be sworn in by Town Clerk Flo Ann Dango.

Thirty-two vote counters raised our right hands and swore (or affirmed) to carry out our duties in keeping with the laws of the state of Vermont.

Our first duty was to unfold the ballots and set them in piles of fifty each. In Weathersfield, one thousand and one people out of eighteen hundred and twelve registered voters cast ballots on November third.

Now to political junkies and students of government, that two-thirds participation rate in an off-year election is cause for celebration.

But to a vote counter, it's a nightmare.

You see, that total meant there were one thousand and one twenty-two-by-fourteen-inch yellow sheets, each containing sixty choices for fifteen state and county offices. And one thousand and one white sheets, each with fifteen nominees for justice of the peace, from which voters were to choose up to ten; and blue sheets, and beige and green sheets, and, finally, one thousand and one blinding hot pink sheets.

For half an hour we unfolded, counted, stacked, recounted, and then turned the piles of ballots over to the boss of the whole operation, Justice of the Peace Lil Daniels.

At about eight o'clock we got down to the real work, paired up one Democrat with one Republican, four people per table. The room grew quiet as the stacks of ballots were distributed.

I was paired with Tom Ballam. When we got our fifty yellow ballots he picked up the pencil and the tally sheet. I began, slowly, clearly, methodically, to read. Leahy, I read, and he found Leahy on the tally sheet and made a mark.

Sanders, I read. He found Sanders and marked. Dwyer. Snelling. Douglas. Milne. And so on.

You find the pace that suits your partner. You find the decibel level he can hear just above the cacophonous roll call that fills the room.

You wonder if you'll ever finish counting this stack.

What you really don't want is to find, as you tally up the hatchmarks after you've read the names from the last sheet in the pile, that the total for any one office is forty-nine, or fifty-one. Because if it's not fifty, you and your partner will go back through every sheet until you rectify the mistake.

You'll do this because you and everybody in this room and in every room like this takes this tedious exercise very seriously. You could, you remind yourself as you call out name after name, with just one misstated total alter some tiny bit of the course of history.

The really neat part of counting ballots is that you get to spend a few seconds in the minds of your fellow citizens. You meet unvarnished minds, unselfconscious about how they'll appear to others, not second-guessing themselves. A bit raw.

So I'm reading to Tom from a ballot: Dean-Racine-Douglas-Markowitz-Flanagan. It all hangs together. A dyed-in-the-wool Democrat.

Then suddenly, in the column for Attorney General, this anonymous voter breaks ranks and picks Grassroots candidate Sandy Ward. You want to stop. You want to find this voter and ask, how'd you decide that?

But you can't pause to ponder the anomaly. You still have seventeen sheets in this stack alone, another hundred and fifty-five names to tally.

The next one picks a Libertarian for governor, a Democrat for lieutenant governor, and the Liberty Union candidate for treasurer.

A few ballots later, a voter calls for Republicans Ruth Harvie and Patricia Welch to be joined by Democrat Cheryl Rivers in the State Senate. What's up here?

You wonder at the logic of some patterns. Then you recall elections when you yourself zigzagged across party lines, and wrote in obscure long shots. And you recall that your reasoning seemed sound, no matter how weird the pattern might have appeared to the vote counters.

As the evening wears on, you grasp the big picture. But it's a very different big picture from the ones the pundits'll use to analyze the election.

Counting those votes, you become less interested in the totals than you are in the idiosyncratic independence the ballots reflect. Counting votes you see democracy not as a grand ideal, but as a collection of sketches: sketches drawn with X's by individuals, one by one pondering in the privacy of the voting booth.

LESSONS FROM THE HURRICANE

THE FEW ACRES we bought when we moved to Weathersfield in 1985 seemed almost perfect.

There was enough lawn by the house for badminton. Behind the house was an acre of white pines that had seeded themselves thirty years before, when what had been fields were subdivided and sold.

To the west were a few acres of fairly mature maple, ash, birch, and cherry. Ferns grew here that, by mid June, would turn the space beneath the forest canopy bright emerald. A brook glinted silver till it dried up in August.

Crossing the stone wall on the western edge of the hardwood grove, you entered a mature evergreen forest.

First came the white pines. The largest rose a hundred feet skyward; they were thick and gnarled. From time to time, a huge rotted spire would crack off in strong winds, and "whump" to the forest floor.

Beyond the pines, just as the land began to rise steeply, you entered a dark hemlock forest.

A deer path ran diagonally up the hill through younger trees to a grove of mature hemlocks. These seventeen trees, some almost nine feet in circumference, encircled a decaying stump, a snag that rose almost ten feet, then tapered into a flamelike wave of still-sinewed wood.

One year I began to visit this grove regularly. I wanted to get to know the insects that lived in the snag, the algae, fungi, and lichen that grew on it, the squirrels who stored provisions in its hollows. I wanted to learn about the trees surrounding it, the few ferns and stunted striped maple that grew in the grove's darkness.

So every few days I walked across the lawn, through the hardwoods, over the stonewall, through the pines, into the hemlocks, and up the hill.

I'd sit, sometimes for hours, watching, listening.

Deer would browse without even noticing me. Once a hawk chased a squirrel through the canopy above me for what seemed an eternity. Spiders waited for black flies to get gummed in their webs. Bits of bark fell from the snag, and ants dug new tunnels, spewing sawdust on the spongy forest floor.

I wanted to chronicle the small changes that took place day after day, season after season in this mini-ecosystem.

Last September, my little wonderland collapsed.

Remember Hurricane Floyd?

My wife and I listened all night to the thrashing and cracking from the forest. We thought we'd wake up to a landscape littered with broken limbs and a few already-dead trees toppled.

But when I entered the forest the next morning, I saw devastation. Mature ash and maple were uprooted, mats of earth and stone and roots tipped up, some as wide as ten feet across. Maybe a dozen trees were downed in two acres.

This was nothing compared to what had happened on the hillside, though.

There, a half acre of forest had been totally destroyed. Where the white pines had met the hemlocks, nothing remained standing. Thick pines were snapped, some at the base, others twenty feet up. Others had been uprooted, and in their toppling had brought down everything in their path.

I looked up.

The dark underbelly of the hemlock canopy was replaced by blue sky. Bright sun shone onto a haphazard stack of trunks and branches and root systems.

Farther up the hillside, my hemlock snag was collapsed, just a small mound of punk and bark where the day before had stood an intricate world I was only beginning to understand.

It's been almost a year since the disaster.

The dead trees have dropped their needles, and now the sun strikes places that have not felt its direct warmth for decades.

I cut a new path around the detritus. I walk it almost every day, pausing to see what's growing and what's not in this new clearing.

The perfect world we bought in 1985 is abruptly changed. I cut and split the hardwood for the woodstove. The rest—all those shattered and crashed pines and hemlocks—I'll just watch.

This is Nick Boke, learning pretty humbling lessons about permanence and transience in Weathersfield, Vermont.

Alan Boye is a professor of English at Vermont's Lyndon State College, where he teaches writing and literature. His writing is both broad and deep, taking in nonfiction, fiction, and drama. Currently, his books include Holding Stone Hands—On the Trail of the Cheyenne Exodus, *and* The Complete Roadside Guide to Nebraska. *Recent nonfiction includes pieces in* Vermont Magazine, Wild West, Yankee, Southern Humanities Review, *and the* Old Farmer's Almanac.

Alan is now at work on a book about an isolated desert in New Mexico known as "The Journey of Death." (AUTHOR PHOTO BY DAVID BOYE.)

THE VICTORY BRANCH

THE VICTORY BRANCH, that's what they called it: eleven miles into the center of one of the wildest areas of Vermont. Someday, everyone thought, the Victory Branch would continue on up over the mountains all the way to Island Pond, far to the north.

At its peak, back at the turn of the twentieth century, the Victory Branch Railroad hauled lumber from mills all over northeast Vermont's Victory Basin. Oh sure, the railroad carried some passengers too. Folks who lived up this way could hop into the single passenger car and ride it on into St. Johnsbury, but lumber was its main cargo.

Now, nearly a hundred years later, the abandoned Victory Branch Railroad makes an ideal pathway for a winter's walk. The old railroad route is a clear, level trail along the banks of the wild Moose River.

I cross the frozen river on a narrow, sturdy footbridge. Bridge Number 116, to be exact. Although the bridge has a new surface, this was the original crossing for the railroad. I lean over the railing and admire a pair of massive granite abutments: large, rough-hewn blocks of stone the color of wood ash.

At any other time of the year I would be distracted by nature's handiwork, but I like it here in winter because the barrenness makes it easier for me to see the traces of the human history.

In front of me, for example, I can easily see the old rail bed. The flat, snow-dusted path of the Victory Branch Railroad enters an arch of dark trees looking for all the world like the entrance to a tunnel.

The trees are a typical Vermont mixture of red spruce, fir, and yellow birch, but they're not the reason I am here. I am here to see the remnants of humankind's growth.

And off to the right I see just such a reminder. A crossed pair of rails poke up through the snow, their black, straight metal edges cleared of summer's tangle of growth. Although the junked locomotives from the Victory Branch were collected for scrap metal during World War Two, if you look carefully you can still find other artifacts, like these rails.

I have always been attracted to the mystery of humankind's presence. And here, near the heart of wild Vermont, winter exposes sets of clues to the riddle. This path is as straight and level as a ruler, as true and precise as the day—over a hundred years ago—some surveyor stood here and plotted the railroad's course through the woods.

The Moose River in this section tumbles down out of Victory Basin in a series of churning rapids and still pools. I walk past one such pool, covered with a white circle of snow, and crisscrossed with otter tracks. Somewhere under that blanket, brook trout are passing the winter in safety, but come spring, they'll rise to fishing lines tossed to them from my path.

The frozen pool ends at sizzling, tumbling, ice-crystaled rapids. Even these rapids provide clues to the presence of humankind. These very rapids provided the power for the sawmill Calvin Morrill built in 1880. I leave the level path and scramble down a short but steep bank to the river's edge, and there it is.

On the other side of the river—just where the tail end of the rapids slows down and surrenders again to winter's icy grasp—is a massive wall of granite blocks. It is a masterpiece of a human artifact. Each of the blocks is the size of a refrigerator, and they fit together like the pieces of a puzzle. The blocks fit so tightly that a slip of paper would barely slide between them.

With just a little imagination I can see the paddlewheel of Calvin Morrill's mill lifting up the silver waters of the churning Moose River. I look from the mill back up to the woods, and what I see there surprises me more than if it had been a hissing steam locomotive. On the flat railroad bed stands a buck, its pronged antlers crowning its head like the smokestack of a train. A veil of snow falls from a tree overhead. In an instant the buck is gone, a puff of smoke in the air.

The Victory Branch Railroad served seven villages, three post offices, five schools, a starch factory, a granite quarry, four railroad stations, a hotel, and six lumber mills.

Someday—everyone thought—someday the Victory Branch railroad would be the very jewel of the Basin. My human forebears believed that the Victory Branch would carry future generations into the light of progress and wealth. As I look at the cookie-cutter prints the buck has left behind on the snow, I decide the Victory Branch Railroad has done just that.

THE VIEW FROM THE DEVIL'S HILL

IT'S THE DEVIL'S OWN HILL, they say. Walk up here and you'll be walking on Satan's property. Given this skinny, gray rain slithering from a sky as misty as midnight, I think there may be some truth in the stories about this hill.

I zip up my rain jacket, peel off my glasses—which are already covered in moisture—and at the darkest of noon hours, I start up the trail to Devil's Hill.

There's not another soul on this trail. No other cars were parked at the end of the twisting, black, narrow trace of a road which serves as the access to the trail head, and there are no footprints between the gray granite slabs which litter the path. I am alone here. As a matter of fact, since Devil's Hill is in the most isolated corner of Groton, Vermont's largest state park, there's probably not another soul for miles in any direction.

I'm not going to think about it. Instead, I study the route ahead. The trail climbs up a long-abandoned logging road. Erosion has made the road into a rocky natural staircase no longer fit for any mechanical beast.

I squint through the trees, trying to catch a glimpse of Devil's Hill. The dark forest blocks my view and adds to the feeling of isolation.

I keep telling myself that it does a body good to be alone every once in a while. Being alone allows you to take stock of yourself. Being alone provides an opportunity for a little serious self-reflection. But today every time I turn my mental gaze inward, I just plain don't like what I see.

This area near Devil's Hill has always been harsh to its human visitors. Maybe this trail—back during the French and Indian Wars—is the very one that the Indians used to lead more than one hundred Massachusetts captives deeper into the wilderness. Since then this hillside has been racked by devastating forest fires, and hurricanes and tornadoes and blizzards.

I almost miss the left turn off the logging road which marks the true ascent of Devil's Hill. I pass through a marshy low dip and then the trail heads upward into the black, drizzly sky. Although it isn't a difficult climb, I find myself huffing and puffing and I stop to catch my breath.

The deep electric smell of skinny rain on dark forest earth; the whisper of mist falling through leaves of ash and maple; the shroud of shadow clouds across the bulk of Devil's Hill in front of me; the nagging insistence of my own pounding heart. I should be rejoicing in nature's isolation, but instead, the regrets of my life tick off like the drops of rain from the brim of my cap: words, un-said; love, unreturned; time—precious, beautiful time—tossed away like sand on some endless beach.

Leaves rustle and I spin around to catch the glimpse of a small bundle of black scurrying into the underbrush. I hurry on up the trail.

The final hundred yards to the top of Devil's Hill is a steep scramble requiring the use of the hand-holds of branches and the slippery treachery of slick rocks. I almost fall backward when I see, punched into this steep slope, the sharp shapes of a cloven hoof.

I clear the last ten feet of this nightmare, step onto the flat smoothness of a granite altar, and abruptly I am at the top.

I stand upright in the suddenly clear space. For a moment the clouds lift. The view is spectacular: The far horizon, a black and gnarled ridge line, develops out of the fog like a photograph. The slate-gray disk of Peacham Pond emerges from the valley floor, and there, straight down, five hundred feet below my boot tops, the thick, suffocating green of Peacham bog.

But just as suddenly, the dismal weather engulfs the ridge line, and seals off the valley below me. One by one the hilltops that remain in view are shut out like souls vanishing from a graveyard.

The name for this pinnacle of stone came about hundreds of years ago when a man, taking a shortcut to his home, crossed this ridge and saw a gigantic black bird hovering over the crown of the hill. He swore to anyone who would listen that he had seen the devil himself. Ever since, this has been Devil's Hill.

I shudder in the dampness. And the devils of my own conscience dance before me again. I want to run from these Lucifers of my own making, I want to deny their existence, to pretend that I just can't see those black-winged shapes in the wilderness of my own soul. But I also know that in order to be able to walk in beauty, every once in a while we all have to take a good look at the view from the top of Devil's Hill.

SUBMIT ADAMS

SUBMIT. THAT WAS THE NAME she was given, and that is the name she was cursed with for a lifetime. Submit. Submit Adams.

Today I am paying her a visit. Though her burial place is not far from the road, the small cemetery is hidden by a beautiful stand of Scotch pines and mixed hardwoods. The path to her grave is nearly invisible in the clutter of leaves. When you walk here, the ground seems like a gentle sponge, and with each step you release a tiny spray of the forest's foam.

We know nothing more about the life of Submit Adams than this: Submit Purchase Adams was the first woman to settle in the Passumpsic Valley and live out her days here. She was probably an Indian, or at least part Indian. She was the wife of the area's first settler: a soldier who fought in the revolution. Submit and her husband pioneered their way into Vermont just after the war.

Submit raised her four sons in a cabin not far from the Moose River. She lost three of those sons to the pioneer spirit. They moved on, building homes further and further into the vast American wilderness.

Submit died in 1797 and was buried on land she had helped change from wild forest to pastures green. Out on a finger of that land, in a pretty spot that looked down over a brook to the Moose River, Submit lies in the family's small cemetery plot.

That is all we know of Submit Adams's life.

Walking the last twenty yards to her cemetery involves a short climb up a steep bank. Useful stone steps have been set into the ground, but they are covered with the debris of a century of trees. The last step takes me to the small, shaded place where she lies.

A few tall, slender tombstones face forward. The one on the left, the darkest one, is hers. It reads:

Mrs. Submit Adams
Departed this Life
November 13, 1797
Age 61 years

Submit Adams. Every time this woman was greeted, every time this woman was needed, every time her husband called to her the same word rang out: "Submit! Submit!"

Did she always obey the command, this woman of native blood held captive in a settler's gown? Did she submit her will, or did she fight for its freedom?

There are perhaps eight or ten burials here at her cemetery. Many of the stones are tipped back toward the earth from where they came.

Nevertheless, it is a lovely spot for a cemetery, for here we are in the heart of the hills of Vermont. Here autumn bows down for its grand display. Here the blast of winter rattles through the skeleton of branches. Here—perched on those branches—a chorus of newly arrived birds announces spring's long-due rebirth. And here summer shows its green and golden glory.

At what once must have been a gate to the cemetery stand two of those sage, ancient maples you could just sit and look at for hours. The gigantic, soft-gray limbs lift hands of branches to the sky. It is not just to remember Submit Adams that we visit her grave. These beautiful maples too are why we are here. What right do we have to demand submission of anyone, we who will last for fewer years than these branches here above us?

This is indeed a holy place. Those of us who love nature, and those of us who love what is good in humankind, pause here to remember the courage of Submit Adams.

Joe Citro has been recording commentaries for Vermont Public Radio since 1992. His work concentrates on the dark side of Vermont's past, its quirks, historical oddities, and supernatural tales.

Since his first literary appearance in 1987, he has published ten books, including five Vermont-based novels of suspense and dark fantasy, three collections that may not be fiction, a book of regional humor, and a guidebook. His novel Shadow Child *is currently in development as a motion picture.*

Joe's collections of Vermont lore serve as a repository for stories that might otherwise be lost or forgotten. His novels, nonfiction books, public appearances, and his work on VPR have done a lot to keep Vermont's past—both real and legendary—alive in the popular culture.

He has taught at Vermont colleges, lectured widely, and has appeared on radio and television all over the country. (AUTHOR PHOTO BY DIANE E. FOULDS.)

THE NEW ENGLAND FAT MEN'S CLUB

BACK IN NOVEMBER of 1903, Jerome Hale, proprietor of Hale's Tavern in Wells River, Vermont, enjoyed a moment of inspiration. He noticed that he, and the ten men clustered around his fireplace, were all conspicuously obese.

The men's cheerful, self-effacing conversation led Mr. Hale to suggest they organize what he dubbed "The New England Fat Men's Club." His portly companions loved the idea.

They all agreed to recruit new members and to meet twice a year. To qualify, one had to weigh at least two hundred pounds. By the time of their fall 1904 meeting, this novel fraternal order had attracted one hundred and ten qualified members.

Many people were eager to join a club that encouraged its members to make the most of themselves. However, certain marginal members had to take drastic measures to stay qualified. For example, Judge Baldwin's trick was to begin stuffing himself the moment he received a meeting announcement. And Frank Sibley hung two horse hitching weights on his suspenders.

Others found the qualifications far easier. A Franklin Falls man weighed an enviable four hundred pounds, but Arthur Moulton of Portland, Maine, carried the most poundage. He weighed in at four hundred thirty-five pounds. Later, with the encouragement of his peers, Mr. Moulton attained a magnificent four hundred seventy-three pounds.

A typical meeting would commence with a ceremonial weigh-in. Then an afternoon of sporting events began on the tavern lawn. David Wilkie won the one-hundred-yard dash, but he had only one opponent. By the time the two men stopped running, it had become a two-hundred-yard dash. They had to cancel the tug-of-war because the rope broke and the men fell. Next year they replaced it with a chain, and competitors soon discovered they could tug just as well sitting down.

Mr. Hale himself won the potato race. But he was accused of having an unfair advantage. At just two hundred and seven pounds he was the only player who was able to see the potato when it was between his feet.

A team could win at baseball in two ways: by total score or by total poundage. In 1905 the winning team excelled at both, with fifteen runs—and 2,279 pounds. The winners had invented ingenious ways of streamlining the game, like taking shortcuts from first to third base.

Some people suggested a pole-vaulting competition, but the idea was scrapped out of respect for the poles. As always, Mr. Wentworth of Somerville, Massachusetts, won his favorite athletic event, the pie-eating competition.

A business meeting followed. Officers were elected, but the main function of the meeting was to alert members that they only had an hour until dinner.

Mr. Hale routinely outdid himself with lavish banquets. Each table was concavely contoured to accommodate the sitter, and the highly caloric nine-course feed virtually guaranteed each man would find the experience broadening.

If any time remained after dinner, there were speakers and other entertainment. But nothing was ever permitted to impede the flow of nonstop hilarity.

The press loved the organization, publicized it, and contributed many well-rounded members to the roster. Over the years, the club's membership expanded. By 1910 enrollment had reached three thousand. By 1925 New England could no longer contain the Fat Men's Club. Membership had reached ten thousand individuals, from thirty-eight states.

People went to great lengths to attend meetings. A man from York Beach, Maine, persuaded a train to make an unscheduled stop by saying "a large party wanted to board." When the train arrived, the four-hundred-thirty-pound Samuel Drew climbed on.

Alas, times changed and membership dwindled. Fewer than forty members attended the twentieth anniversary meeting. Of them, only three were *founding* members. In 1927—the year Jerome Hale died—the New England Fat Men's Club died too.

And that, at least to my mind, was the end of an era.

[Author's note: For additional information, please see Katherine Blaisdell's wonderful *Over the River and Through the Years*, *The Boston Globe*, and various local newspapers of the time.]

THAT MYSTERY GIRL

I WONDER IF New Hampshirites from Coos County recall the odd and poignant events from the summer of 1979?

During July the nine hundred or so citizens of Stewartstown began to hear about a strange—possibly supernatural—visitor.

Events began on July 6 when two young girls, Alberta Buffington and Jean Ann Appleby, were walking near the Stewartstown Hollow School. Suddenly they heard a distressing sound coming from the dark woods behind the building. It was the sound of someone crying.

Naturally concerned, the girls peered into the shadows. There, sitting on a rock at the treeline, was a little girl in a white party dress. She wore ribbons in her hair and another around her waist. She looked about eight years old.

Though Alberta and Jean Ann had never seen this girl before, they wanted to help. But the moment they spoke, the strange little girl fled deeper into the woods.

The two young women didn't dare follow. Soon they became distracted by other things and forgot the whole odd incident.

Then, on July 8, Alberta and Jean Ann saw the same little girl again. She was at the edge of the forest, crying miserably. This time, cautiously and silently, they approached her. But as before, the child vanished among the trees. This time the girls' sympathy turned to fear.

On July 9 they had another encounter. Now the little girl looked pale. Her party dress appeared wrinkled and dirty. A near-panic seized the young witnesses. They ran home and told their parents, who immediately reported everything to Burleigh Placey, Stewartstown's Chief of Police.

But the chief was already on the case.

It seems other people had reported encounters with the same mysterious child. But no one could get close to her. She'd always vanish like a wraith.

A motorist said he heard cries coming from the woods. He stopped to investigate, but saw nothing.

Clara Denton, who lived near the forest, had seen bushes moving and—for three nights running—heard terrifying cries from the depths of the woods. So weird she couldn't describe them, all she could say to a reporter from the *Coos County Democrat* was that "it was a real funny sound."

Folks weren't ready to start calling her a ghost, but no one wanted to think there was a lost or abandoned child in their midst. As Charles Jordan, editor of *Northern New Hampshire Magazine*, told me, every one started referring to her as simply *"that mystery girl."*

After two more weeks of sightings, the pattern remained unchanged: That mystery girl refused to communicate. When anyone approached, she'd disappear.

Chief Placey led local volunteers along with Fish and Wildlife workers on several searches of the area. They found no trace of their elusive little visitor.

After a month of sightings, the media began calling that mystery girl "the ghost of Stewartstown Hollow."

Then came a glimmer of light. A couple from Manchester were planning to build a house in the area. They'd been visiting—along with their daughter. But when Chief Placey displayed her photograph, all witnesses agreed that the "suspect" didn't look anything like that mystery girl.

A general unease increased as weird noises and eerie encounters continued.

By now the population had separated into three groups: believers, nonbelievers . . . and witnesses. Witnesses and believers were certain that that mystery girl was a ghost. Nonbelievers called her a hallucination. But whatever she was—with no clues and no missing persons reports—she remained unidentified.

In the coming months sightings tapered off and eventually stopped. And, little by little, the weird waif of Stewartstown Hollow has slipped from memory.

To this day, more than twenty years later, that mystery girl remains just that—a mystery.

[Author's note: Many thanks to Charles Jordan for recounting stories and furnishing clippings about that mystery girl.]

SPITE CEMETERY

IT HAS OFTEN BEEN SAID that "good fences make good neighbors." If that is true, then Vermont should be one of the most neighborly places around. But don't think for a moment that we don't have our share of disagreements, squabbles, and out-and-out feuds. Perhaps Vermont's answer to the Hatfields and the McCoys would be the Hapgoods and the Baileys, who lived under the shadow of Mt. Ascutney in the tiny town of Reading.

And like all good feuds, this is a tale of willful men, money, land, and perhaps most entertaining of all—an elegant revenge.

It all started around 1770 when Levi Bailey, an enterprising young businessman from Andover, Massachusetts, purchased a parcel of streamside land near the center of town. There he constructed a dam, and built a mill. Its giant wheel was powered by the rushing waters nearby.

Mr. Bailey made money by renting out mill time to local farmers so they could saw wood, grind grist, or spin wool.

Business boomed. But Mr. Bailey didn't want to remain a run-of-the-mill man, so he decided to expand his enterprises. He put in a post office, a tavern, a general store, and even a dance hall. All the time he grew wealthier and wealthier.

He did so well, in fact, that he soon decided to expand again. For years, Mr. Bailey had had an eye on a prime piece of pastureland directly across the brook from his mill.

This coveted parcel was owned by David Hapgood, a farmer who used the land for growing grain and raising sheep. When Mr. Bailey offered to buy the land, Mr. Hapgood straight-out refused.

We can only speculate about why Mr. Hapgood didn't want to sell. Maybe he didn't like flatlanders. Maybe he envied Mr. Bailey's success. Maybe he was peeved about the terrible tectonic crunch of the grindstone, and the piercing screech of the saw blade. Or maybe he was cranky from sleep deprivation due to music and laughter from the dance hall.

In any event, the stubborn David Hapgood repeatedly refused every one of Mr. Bailey's many offers to buy the land.

With each rejected offer, Mr. Bailey's frustration grew. Still, Mr. Hapgood wouldn't budge. Finally the mill owner gave up, but not without issuing something that sounded very much like a threat. "You can't live forever," he shouted at his neighbor. "I'll have that land sooner or later."

Mr. Hapgood's response was a clever one, befitting an obstinate old Vermonter. He donated the coveted streamside land to the town of Reading. The one proviso was that it be used, now and forever, as the town cemetery. At the dedication the town dubbed it "Hapgood Cemetery"—as it is still called today.

This action must have miffed merchant Mr. Bailey in pretty good shape. Now the first thing he saw in the morning, and the last thing he saw at night, was the land he knew he could never own.

When the bullheaded David Hapgood finally died in 1829, he was buried where Mr. Bailey could see his stone, a constant reminder that even in death David Hapgood still possessed the property. And he would do so for all eternity.

And that's why Hapgood Cemetery in Reading, Vermont, is often referred to as "Spite Cemetery."

Fortunately, this story of the feuding neighbors has, I suppose, a happy ending:

Although he had been outfoxed by a crafty old Yankee, Mr. Bailey finally did get *a bit* of the land he had always wanted.

In the year 1850, when Mr. Bailey himself died at age eighty-five, he was buried in his own plot in Hapgood Cemetery. In death Levi Bailey rests just six tombstones down from his lifelong adversary, David Hapgood.

And so, at long last, peace was finally restored between the two rival neighbors.

Although a talented actor and singer, young Will Curtis was in line to run the family shoe manufacturing business—the Curtis Shoe Company—in Marlborough, Massachusetts, when the factory was sold in 1953. Will and his wife Jane promptly moved to West Hartford, Vermont, and bought a dairy farm for $9,000. It turned out to be a natural.

Will was elected to the Vermont Legislature in 1960. At about the same time, he and Jane opened the Yankee Bookshop in Woodstock. Together, they began to write books, including Times Gone By, The World of George Perkins Marsh, *and* Return to These Hills. *From these books and a lifelong love of the environment, Will and Jane drew material for "The Nature of Things," a daily public radio commentary series with listeners across the country. And in a fitting end to this cycle of creation, the syndicated commentary series turned eventually back into books, two collections called* The Nature of Things *and* The Second Nature of Things.

Twenty years later, Will remains one of the most familiar and beloved voices on Vermont Public Radio.
(AUTHOR PHOTO BY JAMIE COPE.)

GRANDFATHER'S BIRTHDAY

THE FOURTH OF JULY was especially exciting when I was young. Of course, my friends and I were up early with a good supply of firecrackers to set off on neighbors' front lawns or in drain pipes attached to their houses. No restrictions in those days! There was a constant din in my part of town as long as the firecrackers lasted. But the best part of the day was my grandfather's birthday.

He was born on the Fourth of July. By late afternoon, our family, brothers and sisters, cousins, aunts and uncles, had gathered at my grandfather's farm to celebrate his birthday. Lake Farm, where he lived in summer, had green lawns sloping down to the water, and around the lawns were pastures filled with Grandfather's prize Guernsey cattle.

My great-grandmother, his mother, had been a notable gardener, and her delphiniums, in every shade of blue, still grew in the gardens. It was a beautiful place.

The house, built in the early 1800s, had had wide porches added at the back of the house overlooking the lake, at the turn of the century. They were called piazzas back then and were filled with old-fashioned, creaky, wicker furniture. But on the Fourth of July, a long table was set with a long linen table cloth, with bouquets of Great-Grandmother's delphiniums. In the center of the table stood a big brass cannon, a family heirloom. It looked huge to me.

Of course we had the traditional New England feast of salmon and peas, and every year some relative would be sure to remind us children that the salmon represented the British Red Coats and the peas symbolized the cannonballs we fired at them. Then came the ice cream and strawberry shortcake.

My cousins and I usually behaved pretty well during this long feast, for we knew what was coming when it got dark: "the night works," as they were called, when rockets would burst overhead and the ground trembled. While we youngsters waited for dark, we were given sparklers to occupy us while the farm hands were putting the fireworks in place down by the lake.

We older boys showed off to the younger cousins, seeing how far we could toss the sparklers in the air and have them still be burning when they came down.

I was bent on outdoing them all, and as a result, mine ended up sputtering away in the branches of a pine tree.

"Fire!" came the call, and the farmhands brought ladders and pails of water. I was humiliated, my older brothers told me just how stupid I had been, but my cousins considered me a bit of a hero for the commotion I had caused.

All the fuss was forgotten when we saw the farm workers with torches, and we knew the big moment had come. As we sat on the lawn watching the rockets explode out over the lake, I thought that nothing could ever be more beautiful.

But there was more to come.

My oldest brother, John, wheeled out the brass cannon and primed it for the big blast. Hands on the lanyard, a cord with a small hook on the end for the firing, he awaited the signal for the end of the day.

And then it came, the last explosion of the fireworks, then my father's voice yelling, "Fire!" and a moment later the roar of the cannon. As we had said the year before, we said again, "This was the greatest show! There never, never, will be any better!"

Looking back through all these years, my only regret is that I never got a chance to pull that lanyard!

CHRISTMAS

IN THE EVENING, when we had our herd of Jersey cows, before heading for bed, I would go out to the barn to put out a little more hay. On Christmas Eve I would linger a bit, for I had been told that on that night all the animals would talk. Unfortunately, there was never any sound but perhaps a few gentle moos.

People still half believe in the magical powers of animals, not just that they are able to talk, but that they kneel in their stalls at the supposed hour of the birth of the Christ Child.

Shakespeare writes of the "Bird of Dawning that singeth all night long so hallowed and so gracious is the time."

We still cherish beliefs in the magic of Christmas. When I hung my stocking by the fireplace, I was thrilled to find it filled with presents. The glass of milk that I had carefully put out was gone, and only some crumbs remained in the saucer where I had put a cookie.

Both Jane's and my family had a tradition that you didn't put up a tree until Christmas Eve. While working in our woodlot, I would keep my eye open for just the right tree and on Christmas Eve afternoon the family would gather to hike up to the woods. There was usually some argument about my choice, but eventually we'd gather around the tree and sing the old German song, "O Tannenbaum." Most of us didn't know the words and just sang "O Christmas Tree, O Christmas Tree," but there was always someone in the family who would show off by loudly singing the German words.

Then the youngest would take a swipe with the ax, small hands being guided by older ones. Then I, being the oldest, would make the last blows, and down the tree would come.

One year after we had sold the herd, and feeling rather lost without the cows, we decided to spend the holidays in London. There was plenty of Ye Olde Christmas cheer about the city, but Father Christmas rather than Santa Claus was the patron saint.

Carolers were everywhere in the week before the 25th, singing under our windows, obliging us to toss coins down to them. We couldn't have Christmas without a tree, and going to a market we were surprised to find only scraggly little trees torn up by the roots. Perhaps we hadn't gone to the proper upper-class market. Anyway we took one home to our little flat and decorated it with bits of cotton wool and bright paper.

That Christmas Eve was one we'll never forget. We went to the midnight service at Westminster Abbey. In the dim, candlelit Abbey, the choir voices soared high among the vaulted arches above our heads. We were sure that we had heard the angels singing. Next day we went with most of London to the Zoo. The English are famous for their love of animals, and Londoners are convinced that the zoo animals need a little treat for Christmas. No use telling them that the zookeepers are expert at animal nutrition. So we walked through the cold, damp London streets to Regent's Park Zoo, carrying what bits and pieces we had left over from our Christmas dinner. We joined the good-hearted citizens in holding out a slice of plum pudding to an elephant who seemed to appreciate it and an orange to a monkey. But the zebra spurned a cracker, turned around and kicked his stall. Still, we felt that we had done our best as Americans who no longer had cows to feed.

MAPLE SUGARING TIME

⌀

MANY OF US that milked cows anxiously waited for the sun in late February or early March to warm our sugar bush. Sugaring time is those days between winter's icy embrace and the time when maple buds redden and swell. The nights are below freezing, but when the sun appears over the hills in the east the temperature quickly rises.

That is the time when farmers gladly leave the barn and head for the woods. It's almost like having a vacation.

"I think it's about time to tap, heard John's tractor up in his bush yesterday." So we would collect the buckets and lids, hammers and bits and drills, and gather the spiles in buckets, and get the snowshoes, and up the tractor would go though the pasture to the sugar bush.

There's a trick to tapping; you don't want to put too many buckets on young trees and overstress them. When you come to a mature maple you look up into the crown to see where the branches are thickest; that's where the greatest amount of sap will be likely to flow.

We drilled with a 7/16-inch bit, drilling at a slight upward angle. Then we'd hammer in the spile, hang the bucket and slide on the lid, and head for the next tree. Of course I'm talking about how it was in the old days before plastic tubing made everything much easier. But I wonder if today's sugarmakers have as much fun as we did.

There is nothing so heady as a beautiful day in March when you can almost hear the sap rising and the sun is shining. We would go from tree to tree, emptying the sap buckets into those buckets we had hanging from shoulder yokes. We would dump these into the gathering tank behind the tractor. When we'd made the rounds we'd drive the tractor to the sugarhouse and, attaching a pipe, drain the contents of the gathering tank into the holding outside.

During the fall, a large pile of wood would have been collected. When there was enough sap to start boiling, the pans inside the house would be filled by a pipe from the holding tank, the arch fired up, and the delicate art of turning sap into syrup would commence.

Sugaring is indeed an art. One moment's inattention, and the syrup burns and catches fire and a very expensive pan will be ruined. The sugarmaster must calculate the exact moment the sap has thickened to syrup and then draw it off into containers.

It was hot work firing the arch; you could never let the temperature drop down. We took turns at that job, the firer wearing a heavy leather apron and thick gloves and with a face as red as the fire in the arch. We'll never forget those days up in our sugar bush. Today with modern techniques and oil-fired arches, sugarmakers are producing a lot more syrup. Each tap now averages a quart of maple syrup. In an orchard with 2,500 spiles the yield can be as much as 626 gallons.

The season usually starts in March and lasts until the third week of April. It varies of course, a great deal, with the onset of an early or late spring. Usually the season lasts about ten to twenty-five days. If the weather suddenly turns warm, the sap stops running until cold temperatures again prevail.

What causes the sap to run? One theory—and there are several—is that when the weather warms up to above thirty-two degrees Fahrenheit, maple sap expels carbon dioxide. The carbon dioxide collects in the fiber that surrounds the vessels that conduct the sap. The expanding carbon dioxide squeezes the vessels, putting pressure on the sap. This same pressure drives the sap up to the point of least resistance.

However it works, we are happy when we pour that sweet syrup over our pancakes on Sunday morning. Or any time.

A VPR commentator since 1998, Peg Devlyn specializes in health topics—no surprise given her background in public policy as both a journalist and a U.S. Senate staffer. She is particularly adept at probing issues for their meaning to real people, and for the roots of their growth and currency as public concerns.

Peg's ample community service—including time as a past president of Vermont Businesses for Social Responsibility, a trustee for the Vermont Land Trust and Fanny Allen Hospital, and a delegate to the Vermont Conference of the United Church of Christ—pales only before her family activities, these including her four children and ten grandchildren. She has served two terms on the Colchester Board of Education.

Peg is co-owner of Marketing Partners, Inc., a Burlington, Vermont, marketing communications firm.

(AUTHOR PHOTO BY ALAN SMITHEE.)

PROZAC FOR CHILDREN?

LOOKING AT THE WORLD through the eyes of a marketing professional can be like looking at a green lawn with your nose pressed down in the grass. There's a lot more going on than you thought, and it's not always pretty.

Recently, I stuck my nose into the topic of drug companies and their marketing plans for our children. Flush with success at peddling Ritalin and other brands of mind control drugs for kids, the pharmaceutical companies are now preparing minty and orange-flavored antidepressants, made palatable for little tikes.

According to a report in *The Wall Street Journal*, companies like Pfizer, Bristol Myers, Squibb, American Home Products, and Eli Lilly, the maker of Prozac, see a rich new market in children for antidepressants. They need the kids to help make up for slowing growth in the huge adult market for drugs like Prozac and Paxil.

These drugs, with their marketing blitz of the early nineties, piled up incredible profits for the drug companies. They are among the most commonly prescribed drugs in America. But last year the drug companies had only 17% growth in these antidepressants, to $3.77 billion dollars, compared to 63% growth in 1994, the *Journal* reported. So children are their next target.

This kind of greed cannot hide behind the real needs of a small number of mentally ill children for better treatments.

I only have to look at the abuse of Ritalin and its cousins to worry about a new generation of kids on yet another type of mind and behavior-controlling drug. Ritalin, a central nervous system stimulant with effects similar to cocaine, is given to kids to treat what is called attention deficit disorder. Every day, thousands of Vermont kids line up at their school nurses' office for their midday doses of Ritalin to control them through the day.

The overuse and abuse of Ritalin are just starting to come to light, but nobody knows yet what the long-term effects will be. There's no question that these drugs help calm some children, but at what price? What will the future be for the massive numbers of youngsters whose energy and behavior have been controlled by drugs for years, most often without counseling or other treatment?

So now here comes another pill for kids predicted to have a market as big as Ritalin's. How will we prevent more abuse in this money-driven push to sell more drugs to more millions of kids?

The amount of money for the upcoming marketing onslaught is enormous, and we can expect to see the marketing roll-out soon. It will come in the guise of important health news. Watch for news articles about the extent of juvenile depression and how treatable it is with newly approved drugs. Watch the free samples pour into the doctors' offices, the paid conferences for them at sunny resorts. Katie Couric will interview some drug promoters with initials after their names who will tell us our kids are depressed and their drugs are the answer.

Watch for yet another lineup of medicine cups at the school nurse's office. But don't count on a school full of children now instantly happy and well behaved. The *Journal* quoted Dr. Peter Jensen of the National Institutes of Health: "Pills don't create skills," he said. Children need help with self-esteem, social skills, and other problems no medication can treat.

Who will protect the children? There's no possibility these kids can give informed consent for the huge drug experiment about to be conducted on them. What happens if these drugs permanently alter developing brains? There's no experience with a generation of children treated for several years with mind-altering drugs. Will they emerge from childhood addicted? When and how do they withdraw from these controlled substances?

The only brakes I can see on this scheme are a public opinion backlash and a fear of lawsuits. If I were a beginning law student, I'd start my file now for the generation of lawsuits that will follow tobacco.

VERMONT JOB GAP

IN A BUSINESS PRESENTATION last week, I saw this cartoon: A sign on the workplace wall said, "The beatings will continue until morale improves." We all laughed comfortably.

But recently I learned that even in America, and right here in Vermont, there is a surprising cruelty going on in our workplaces. Here's how it works. Nearly everybody needs a job to survive, and nearly every business needs employees. Government brokers the basic deal and the contract is this: Hire a worker and pay her or him half of what it costs just to get by.

That's the minimum wage. Your employees will not have enough money for food, housing, and health care, but we'll partly subsidize them for you. They may be able to get some food stamps, maybe a little health coverage, a rent subsidy or emergency fuel. Of course, they won't be respected if they use these programs, and they still won't have enough. They'll just work second jobs.

"Sounds like a good deal for them," say the employers. "But we hate paying the taxes for those subsidies. That's why you can't balance the budget. Cut them back."

I hate to believe this is happening in Vermont. We're different here. There's a Yankee value here that says everybody ought to work for a living. And there's a belief to go with that, that everyone who works full time can pay his own way. That's how it should work.

But recently, a blue-ribbon panel of Vermont economists, business leaders, academics, and government and nonprofit representatives released a study called "The Vermont Job Gap." Their purpose was to find out what it really costs to meet a family's basic needs in Vermont, and what wage is needed to meet those basic needs and taxes. They call that the Livable Wage.

The results of the study are stunning. Forty percent of single working adults fail to earn enough money to live on. That goes up to seventy percent for families with one parent and one child. Nearly half of traditional families of two parents (one working) and two children fail to earn a Livable Wage. And it's not much better when both parents work. Thirty-eight percent of those families fall short of a Livable Wage.

The researchers concluded that the lowest Livable Wage in Vermont, providing the basic needs for one person, is $7.98 an hour, with employer-assisted health care. That's the cost here for minimal rent and utilities, food, telephone, health care, transportation, clothing, personal expenses, and renters' insurance. For an adult with one child, the Livable Wage jumps to $12.36, including child care.

These are budgets with nothing for recreation, meals out, gifts, or anything more than the bare necessities. So with so many Vermonters earning less than that, how do they make up the difference? The hard truth is, many cannot, the study says, so they do without necessities. For example, 60,000 have no health care. Some rely on credit cards, creating additional burdens. Some fall back on families or government assistance programs. Often they are cold, hungry, and ill.

This painstaking research finally puts reliable numbers to this issue. It makes it clear that the minimum wage is not even close to a real minimum anyone can live on. It causes cruel hardship for hard-working people. Working for less than a Livable Wage is not earning a living. When our businesses need to depend on minimum-wage workers, they are being subsidized by the taxpayers and by the hardships of the workers themselves. This situation violates our Yankee values.

I think most Vermont small business owners are unaware of this gap. One told me, "I hate that, but I'm trapped. I have to compete with everyone else on the street, and I can't raise prices enough to pay more."

Just as the Job Gap study is a collaboration among business, economic, and other community representatives, the solution also needs a community-wide approach. There are benefits for all of us.

For example, the study says if families earned Livable Wages, tax revenues would rise and the demand for public assistance would decrease. Greater purchasing power would mean businesses would sell more goods and services.

Already, there is tremendous statewide support for making a Livable Wage a Vermont goal. Vermont Businesses for Social Responsibility has adopted the Livable Wage as a goal, and some of its members have begun raising wages to meet its standards.

The Vermont Economic Progress Council's ten-year economic plan calls for bringing Vermont wages up to one hundred percent of the national average. The state also recently created the Vermont Sustainable Jobs Fund, aimed at growing jobs here that pay livable wages.

The gap between actual wages and what it takes to live is a national problem. It's not surprising to me, though, that Vermont is taking the lead in addressing it. In fact, to me, that spirit is the core of why Vermont is such a unique and beautiful place to be.

BIG BOX SCHOOLS

✑

WHILE PEOPLE THROUGHOUT VERMONT are looking for ways to make schools safer, and asking how to reduce education costs, here's a big caution: Don't make schools bigger. Don't even think about merging small schools into big ones, not to save money, not to have grander buildings, not for any reason.

As South Burlington looks at a plan to merge three neighborhood elementary schools into one huge institution with 1,400 young children, and other districts throughout the region study ways to save money with mergers, we need to look at some striking information on the real costs of big box schools. They get failing grades on safety, on quality, and even on cost.

When I hear of a small school closing, I have a sense of losing something precious. But this is not just the intuitive reaction of a parent who loves the notion of small, friendly Vermont schools where everyone knows everyone else and children grow in a warm atmosphere, learn Yankee values, salute the flag, and eat maple sugar. We have research.

Consider safety, on all our minds this year. Overwhelming evidence is mounting fast that small schools are safer than large schools. According to research compiled by the Annenberg Rural Challenge, a national educational group with an office in Randolph, Vermont, five of the seven recent school shootings happened in schools with more than 1,000 students. None happened in a small school.

The Rural Challenge cited several studies showing school size to be the most important predictor of violence in schools at all grade levels. A study of primarily large schools warned that U.S. schools are hotbeds of violence. And Rural Challenge cited a U.S. Department of Education survey of school principals with some telling numbers. Some thirty-eight percent of principals in schools with more than 1,000 students reported serious discipline problems, compared to fifteen percent in medium-size schools and ten percent in small schools.

This year has seen a huge increase nationally in school purchases of metal detectors, hiring of guards, and restriction of student freedoms, primarily at larger schools. Yet studies tell us that in schools where students have fewer rights and more restrictions, violence is increased. Before we move toward creating more larger schools here, with more uniformed guards and weapon checks, we should at least wait for more of the school violence research to be completed.

Still, in the wake of new school funding plans in Vermont and New Hampshire, some people are looking for cost savings by consolidating schools. But taxpayers might be surprised to learn what this idea could really cost them. Start with money. Vermont's Small Schools Study Group found that there is no absolute right size for schools, but the smallest and the largest schools are the most expensive, both nationally and in Vermont.

The Vermont Education Department's Small Schools Report tells us it costs six to twelve percent more to operate schools with fifty or fewer students than schools with a few hundred. But the savings dwindle and then disappear as schools get larger. Higher expenses for the smaller schools come primarily from smaller class sizes, a key factor in both quality and safety.

Let's face it, big box schools have some of the same appeal as big box stores. You can save some money and you get easier parking. You get a big new building with new bells and whistles.

You sacrifice personal service, attention to quality, and a strong local community resource. You increase sprawl and soul-deadening sameness. You honor money more than community. With big box schools, you honor money more than your children.

With a background in both literature and religion, artist Lois Eby views the world from a particularly complex and vivid perspective. She is an accomplished cover illustrator, often matching her designs with books of poetry. In 1999, she was awarded an Opportunity Grant from the Vermont Arts Council to support development of an exciting new series of paintings.

Lois has put together numerous one-person shows, in Vermont and on New York's Lower East Side. She is a member of the adjunct faculty in art of the Adult Degree Program at Vermont College in Montpelier. (AUTHOR PHOTO BY ANDREW Y. KLINE.)

A PASSION FOR ART

THE FIRST TIME I remember falling in love with a painting was in the sixties. As a student, I went to Germany for a summer to work in an office. On a weekend off I traveled to Holland. I still remember climbing up the long wide flight of stairs in the Rijksmuseum, arriving at the top step, and resting my gaze on a painting of sunflowers across the wide landing.

Perhaps it was the long journey to arrive at that place and the long flight of stairs that caused my intense response, but I think it was the yellow, the brilliant and emotional yellow with which Vincent Van Gogh painted those sunflowers. I was struck breathless by his vision of sunflowers, their larger-than-life yellow, his larger-than-life brushstrokes. I stood at the landing, stunned.

I awoke to painting with that experience, and I have been falling in love with one painting after another ever since. But unlike an experience of human romance, I never give up a previous love. I only add to my list, not a list of conquests but of surrenders, in an ever-expanding circle of falling in love.

What is it about visual art that evokes this response? One answer that pops into my mind is that in visual art the physical world and the soul of humanity join and become one. Van Gogh's sunflowers are more than sunflowers, and more than Van Gogh. Color and line have given Van Gogh a language with which to express his feeling for life. His painting of sunflowers becomes a meeting place of the spirit of earth and the human spirit. By entering into his vision, my own life experience is enriched and deepened, as are my experience of color and line, my experience of sunflowers, and my experience of how it feels to be human.

There have been other great moments of falling in love: seeing the watercolors of Paul Cézanne at the Museum of Modern Art in New York, or, at the Boston Museum of Fine Arts, the African American artist John Biggers's magical and deeply spiritual evocations of his people.

I don't remember the first time I saw and began to love Japanese and Chinese ink painting. When I see Gesshu's calligraphy I am breathless; I experience that clutch in the pit of my stomach that I get in the presence of art with which I deeply connect. The swift and rhythmic stroke is rich with the sorrow and joy of each moment. Surrounded as the black ink is by the empty space out of which we all emerge, it's a beauty that touches my heart.

Knowing artists and visiting their studios deepen my response to art, for there above all places one finds love for the materials of art: the colors, the paint, the clay, the wood, even for some the computer graphics program. Artists see possibility in those materials, the possibility of getting at the truth of their experience and expressing it to others and the possibility of contributing to the ongoing effort of all peoples everywhere to express their experience of life in visual form. A true artist gives up everything for the love of the materials and the honesty required for a genuine encounter with those materials. For this, I have come to love not only works of art, but artists themselves.

Ours is rapidly becoming one multicultural world. We have a great need not only to value the creation of works of art from the past, but to be curious about, to allow ourselves to fall in love with, the many different kinds of art that are arising out of this new and changing world. I can't think of anything better than to walk up a great flight of stairs, or into a little gallery space, discover there the honest encounter of an artist with her or his materials, and tumble into love once again.

THE ARTISTS AT "OUT AND ABOUT"

IF YOU WANT to brighten a January day, come with me into the art room at "Out and About," an adult day-care center in Morrisville, Vermont. Here I work with older and disabled artists as they create paintings and sculpture. I am an artist mentor to these artists; I help them solve problems and develop their work.

Right now the room is quiet. The artists have settled down to work for the morning, forgetting the cold outside and sharing instead a common absorption in their various projects. As I move from person to person to see if anything is needed, I often think of other older artists who have painted here over the years.

One of these artists was Maude Holman. Maude was in her nineties when she died. She did delicate paintings of flowers and outdoor scenes. On my way to the "Out and About" studio, I used to pick up flowers at Peck's Flower Shop, which donated a bouquet each week for Maude to paint. I learned something important from Maude. She was tough, and she had high standards. When she was younger, she lived in Boston. She always tried to dress elegantly. She would not settle for anything but the best: a decent brush, a clean palette of watercolors, and good paper. She defended her rights, even in her nineties.

In my home I treasure a small painting by Maude Holman. It is of a bird looking up quizzically at a worm flying past. What makes it special is Maude's quirky sense of humor, her delicate touch . . . and the way the worm flies, while the bird stands rooted in place, surrounded by grass and flowers.

My thoughts also often turn to Doris Moffat. Doris became an abstract painter in her late sixties. She had heart disease and other health problems, but she came to "Out and About" with great zest and seriousness about her painting. Doris painted on slabs of wood, on canvas, on cloth, on paper. Her colors were intense and vibrant. When Doris was painting, one could hardly keep up with her energy. She wanted to try something new; she wanted to show her work. When I feel blue, I can look at Doris's bright, energetic colors on a slab of wood hanging on my wall, think of her courageous, adventuresome spirit, and plunge again into my day.

As I work with other artists around the art table at "Out and About," I continue to remember the way Maude Holman and Doris Moffat started painting late in life and loved having the chance to paint. Like other artists at "Out and About," their lives took on new meaning and purpose when they started painting. An appreciative audience responded to their work. They had something to give others through their paintings.

One thing I notice about older artists who begin painting late in life is that each artist naturally and automatically develops a style that is uniquely his or her own. Unconstrained by formal training, these artists produce work that can be instantly recognized as theirs in a roomful of paintings. This matter of unique style is as miraculous as the fact that snowflakes are all different in form or that we all have different DNA. Left to our own devices, each of us grows into a personality with a vision of our own to share with the world. This vision seems to ripen with age.

Some people look at the paintings and sculptures created by older and disabled artists and see only art that lacks formal training. What I see is the freshness and endless bounty of the human imagination and the uniqueness of each human soul. Working with older artists has given me something that might come as a complete surprise in our time of obsessive focus on youth. I have learned from these artists, more than anywhere else in my life, to appreciate the boundless creativity of the human spirit. Given the opportunity, this creative spirit can spring at a moment's notice onto a piece of paper in an image so fresh, so original, so full of color, that time stands still, and only the human spirit remains.

THE NATIONAL CIVIL RIGHTS MUSEUM

IN THE SUMMER of 1998 my family and I happened to be in Memphis, Tennessee, for a family wedding. One day we took off from the festivities and went to the National Civil Rights Museum, a museum built around the Lorraine Motel where Martin Luther King Jr. was assassinated almost thirty-two years ago.

Does one have to have lived through that terrible day in April 1968 to feel as I did when I saw the balcony where Reverend King was shot? With his assassination, I lost the naive hopes of my youth. I realized that the struggle between good and evil is an ongoing struggle. It will never be won. It requires courage and sacrifice on the part of committed people, year after year, century after century.

I entered the Lorraine Motel with awe. Here was a tribute not only to Martin Luther King, Jr., but also to the many other people who waged the long, hard fight for civil rights.

I first became involved in the civil rights movement as a college student in the early sixties. My deepening commitment to the movement was not entirely altruistic. At the university in the south where I went to school, I discovered that it was against school policy for me to bring a nonwhite friend to eat with me in the cafeteria. My civil rights were being violated. Such infringement on my personal liberty was against everything I had learned about American freedoms when I was growing up in Oklahoma. That's when I understood that civil rights is an issue not only for African Americans but for all of us.

It was a powerful experience to work our way slowly through the civil rights museum, looking at the photographs and reading the history of events. The museum focuses on the fifties and sixties, but reaches much further back in time as well. My daughter searched for and found photographs of a few white women who played courageous roles in the civil rights movement. As we moved along, however, we were aware that there were few other white people in this museum. Busloads of African American children from Memphis schools, African American couples, families, and individuals . . . many people were there, in hushed and reverent awe as we were, but very few white people.

Do white people take their civil rights for granted? Is it location? While the Lorraine Motel is a fitting place for a tribute to Martin Luther King and to the struggle for civil rights, it also seemed to us that this museum, so well conceived and executed, should be invited and helped to open another branch right on the mall in Washington, D.C.

This museum should be at the center of our national life. Civil rights is a national issue. From the moment the founders of our country fought for freedom from England while they encouraged and profited from slavery, our country has been both a symbol of political rights for the individual and a contradictory battleground. The rights of the individual and the greed and prejudice of the majority have been at war. The history of abuse of the civil rights of African Americans, and their fight to obtain their rights, are a part of the American story. We should all know and honor this story. It's about us and who we are as a country. When we hear of horrific abuses of minorities in other countries, we need to know that our country has been and is guilty of such abuse as well. But we also need to be proud that we have a long history of struggle, struggle by heroic African Americans and visionary white men and women, to extend the rights of our Constitution to all our citizens.

So I'd like to see a branch of the National Civil Rights Museum in our nation's capital. We must never forget to honor those in our history who fought to make our country live up to its Bill of Rights, for we need such courageous and committed leadership in every generation.

Ellen David Friedman is, first and last, a political activist. Her political causes, beginning in preadolescence, switching to Harvard and then to Vermont in 1974, are legion: the Vermont Alliance; the Vermont Coalition for Jobs, Peace, and Justice; Vermont Solidarity; the Vermont Rainbow Coalition; the Progressive Coalition; Vermont Progressive Party; Jesse Jackson for President (both 1984 and 1988); and Bernie Sanders for Governor (1986) and Congress (1988–present). She is a dedicated union organizer, with roots in the United Electrical Workers; the American Federation of State, County, and Municipal Employees; and the Vermont National Education Association.

Ellen and her husband Stuart Friedman are thirty-year vegetarians, committed bicyclists, and vipassana meditation practitioners. Apparently, she has been successful in transmitting her passions: Son Eli is a budding student activist and China scholar at Bard College.

(AUTHOR PHOTO BY STUART FRIEDMAN.)

TAKE BACK VERMONT

OKAY. WE'VE ALL SEEN the lawn signs. "Take Back Vermont" sounds like a big idea, but all it really means is take back the legislature for the Republicans. Or at least those Republicans who oppose civil unions. Suddenly this looks like a small idea.

And since I'm one of those many Vermonters who think the civil unions law is both right and necessary, I'm not buying what they're selling.

But then I started thinking, *Aren't there parts of Vermont that I'd like to take back myself?* Absolutely! Here's what I want back:

I'd like to take Vermont back from those transnational corporations that have destroyed our locally controlled economy. The ones who devastated Windsor and Springfield by shipping out good-paying union jobs to cheap labor markets in the impoverished Third World. And the agribusiness monopolies that undercut family farms and decimate rural communities.

I'd like to take Vermont back from the retail conglomerates that can't rest until they've put a Wal-Mart and Home Depot and Costco in every part of the state, destroying our flatlands and Main Streets, and hooking consumers into the highest level of personal debt ever recorded.

I'd like to take Vermont back from the medical-industrial complex—that powerful profit center that includes drug companies, the insurance industry, the medical equipment manufacturers, and the financial interests that get rich on our insurance premiums. These businesses have got us running scared, with no choice but to pay whatever price they demand.

I'd like to take Vermont back—particularly at the dinner hour—from telemarketers. And the advertising industry that squanders millions of dollars to lure kids to cigarettes, or adults to booze, or young women to hating the way they look.

I know what's been taken from us, and I think I know why. What's been taken from many ordinary Vermonters is the sense of well-being. In the middle of this booming economy, lots of us worry about having decent jobs. We worry about how to pay the fuel bills, the dental bills, and the property tax. We're scared of getting sick or not being able to pay the insurance premiums. We find ourselves in debt.

The motive of the real takers is certainly clear: For the corporations it's all profits and power. And I'm not speaking here of garden-variety profits, those made by small and locally owned businesses. I'm talking about the incomprehensibly vast profits and immense concentration of power held by a handful of transnational corporations. And we never elected them, did we? We never invited them to take charge. But we've sure been taken.

Now, I understand that the folks with lawn signs up have a different notion of who's taken Vermont. They insist the legislature has robbed them of local control. But I don't think our legislature is really all that powerful. Certainly not compared to Monsanto, one of the many chemical companies that genetically engineer our food and milk for profit. Not compared to U.S. Healthcare, a for-profit

HMO that paid their CEO a $1 billion bonus, while we struggle to pay our insurance premiums. Not compared to the pharmaceutical industry that waltzed into Montpelier this spring with half a dozen high-paid lobbyists and killed a bill that would have made prescription drugs affordable. Compared to that kind of big-time taking, our legislature is just a sideshow.

There's certainly anger out there, but I wonder if there aren't better targets for it than the legislature. Aren't there other, more practical problems that matter more than civil unions to most Vermonters? I'm thinking of everyday things like good jobs, health care we can afford, excellent schools, strong community services, and a clean environment.

If so, then it's not too late to recognize we have more in common than we've got dividing us. And we should start talking to each other about who has really taken Vermont, and what we can do together to take it back.

GLOBALIZATION

SEVERAL WEEKS AGO the owner of the profitable Stanley Tools plant in Shaftsbury announced he was closing it and shipping the work south. Just like that. No prior discussion with the workers. Two hundred jobs just gone. Two hundred families paying mortgages, meeting loan payments for their kids' college tuition, buying groceries and fuel oil . . . suddenly standing on thin ice. Two hundred skilled workers, some with decades of seniority and excellent wages won by years of contract negotiation, will now be scrambling for the jobs that this so-called boom economy has created—low-paid, dead-end work in retail or tourism. And to add insult to injury, the boss isn't shutting down because Stanley Tools wasn't making him a profit in Shaftsbury; it's just that he can make bigger profits in North Carolina or Mexico.

Shaftsbury and nearby Bennington will absorb this punch in the gut the way towns like Springfield and Windsor have, as machine tool plants there have been dismantled by their corporate owners and the work sent away. They'll absorb it in lost tax revenues, declining property values, reduced local retail, and an increased burden on public assistance. Valuable industrial facilities, with many decades of public subsidy under their belt, will stand vacant and unproductive. And meanwhile we are made to believe that this is simply the inevitable march of economic progress or, by its other name, globalization.

Globalization of course has many faces, and many defenders. There are those who say we all benefit when large transnational corporations move freely across borders. But I think it's an economic strategy that sacrifices too much for growth at any cost.

Globalization can be criticized for many reasons, including the downward spiral of wages, and undercutting of environmental laws. But what really concerns me is how globalization affects our sense of community.

Community is precious to Vermonters. Both the "Take Back Vermont" phenomenon and the brave struggle for recognition of same-sex families can be seen as expressions of this. Whether sixth generation or newcomer, whether left, right, or center, whether gay or straight, it seems we're all yearning for life on a scale that makes sense, a scale where we can work things out together, and control our own collective destiny—not where we are helpless pawns of larger forces. It's our small-town life, not as a picture postcard, but as a living expression of our values, that we want to protect.

But the global economy finds such old-fashioned notions inconvenient. Stanley Tools was a brick in the foundation of Shaftsbury's community life, but the boss doesn't really care if it crumbles. He's not from here, and doesn't have to care. But the rest of us do.

And fortunately, we do have a choice. We can begin insisting that our state policies favor "localization" over globalization. We can put Vermont-owned businesses first in line for tax subsidies from the state. We can foster self-sufficiency by supporting sustainable Vermont enterprises in agriculture, lumber, energy generation, education, and health care. We can, for example, use woodchip by-products from lumber mills to heat schools so we aren't hostage to international oil price-fixing. We can leverage precious public money to invest in Vermont, rather than watching our capital drain away. We can use our government to serve our needs, and to protect and strengthen our rural communities. It's our choice.

THE ASSIGNMENT

MY BEST FRIEND, whose name is also Ellen, has just been diagnosed with acute leukemia. Incredibly, a similar fast-moving bone marrow cancer killed her husband Michael three years ago, just eight months after he had been diagnosed. This is a story about life as it is, not as we wish it to be. Since we all live in this world, a world we don't control, where painful and unbearable things occur, there may be something for each of us to learn from how Michael, and now Ellen, faced the unfaceable.

"I'm sorry I'm making you go through this again," Ellen apologized last week, through her own tears and mine, as she revealed the news about her diagnosis. I was horrified that she would feel the need to apologize, as if my experience was harder than her own.

"This is ridiculous," I told her. "It's my privilege to go through this with you."

But she apologized again a bit later, and then again until I finally got it, and accepted her apology. What she was dismayed by was that lives would be disrupted on her account and, in this way, she was acknowledging the communal nature of what was up ahead. My job was simply to accept the assignment. Four years earlier, Michael had greeted my husband Stuart and me in his kitchen, with the same dizzying news, by saying, "Well, kids, here's our next project."

And that is one great thing we've learned from our two friends: The disease may belong to the individual, but the response can belong to the community. I have to tell you about our community—the group of people in and around Montpelier who've worked on this project. They are extraordinary. They have done, and are now again doing, the most precious kind of public service. There are the ones who become parents to Ellen and Michael's daughter, the ones who take over the finances and legal work, the ones who learn about the disease and its treatments, who advocate within the medical system, who cook, do the laundry, drive. And then there is the next circle out, the friends of friends who find a hundred different ways to be supportive. School counselors, and local business owners, and work colleagues and neighbors make gestures of unutterable loveliness and compassion. Together they produce something that cannot be purchased. They make it safe to go through this.

Paradoxically, it was Michael who set this safety standard for us originally. Somehow he understood that the big job of facing a life-threatening illness had to begin by shedding fear. I'm not talking about being macho, about ignoring fear or fighting fear. I'm talking about the great strength that comes when you accept reality as it is, and choose to live fully, in the present moment. He was a real artist in this regard, and all of us who were nearby benefited. Concretely what this meant was that we didn't waste too much time with regrets. We didn't get angry at a capricious and unjust universe. We didn't get short-tempered with overworked medical personnel, or impatient with insurance adjustors. We didn't mourn the loss of our extended bike trips, or summers at a local pond. We just loved one another and felt lucky to be plumbing the depths of our own capacities. Our available energies went to building the safe and strong community that survives death.

On the night three years ago that Michael, Ellen, Stuart, and I ate dinner together for the very last time, I asked Michael whether there was anything he wished to know, with confidence, would happen after his death. "Can we assure you of anything," I asked, "before you die?"

His answer was so terrific. He said, "My confidence is complete and it has nothing to do with what happens in the future. I'm confident that you will all do what needs to be done. That's enough."

And I think he was right. We do feel equipped to face the challenge of Ellen's life-threatening illness. Of course the sadness is profound, but so is the lively, irrepressible confidence we have discovered in ourselves and within our community. It's all we need.

With a master's degree in education from William and Mary, and after early stints working for Vermont newspapers and for universities here and abroad, Allen Gilbert focused his life on Vermont's educational needs and affairs. In addition to serving on his local and regional school boards, Allen is a past president of the Vermont School Boards Association. He currently works with the Vermont Student Assistance Corp.

Allen's public service also includes a term on the Planning Commission and on the Zoning Board of Adjustment in Marshfield, Vermont. He founded and remains a partner in a writing, research, and publications company that assists mainly nonprofit organizations. In the summer he bikes, in the winter he cross-country skis, and at all times Allen Gilbert dreams of once again setting up his American Flyer model trains in the basement of his house. (AUTHOR PHOTO BY ANDREW KLINE.)

CONNECTING WITH KIDS

IT'S THE END of the year—the school year, that is. And even though the new school year won't start for several months, this is a good time to make a new year's resolution—about schools, and about kids.

The resolution that I wish us all to make is to visit our local schools—at least once during the next school year. Simple, straightforward, easy to do. And possibly of extraordinary significance.

I'm recommending this because whenever I spend time in my kids' school, I come away feeling better about what's going on there, and about what kids are thinking. And, I must admit, I come away sobered to think that we're often not in touch with our kids the way we should be.

Let me give two examples. The other month my local high school had an art show. Work that kids had done during the year was displayed in the halls and classrooms. I was drawn to a group of photographs and short writings titled "Who I Am." First was a photograph that the student had taken, and then a short autobiographical piece. The students were seventh graders. I thought it would be fun to try to see what some of the kids who recently graduated from our local elementary school had written. I was floored by the sensitivity and reflection that I discovered.

"I'm an ordinary girl in the 7th grade," one student wrote. "But to really describe me isn't to tell about the girl who has blue eyes, or what school she goes to, or how tall she is. It's about the girl who loves to laugh, the girl who likes to be unique, the one who thinks being with friends and family is one of the funnest things in the world. I'm a girl who likes to do things, make things happen, a girl who likes to run around until her eyes water from the wind, an active girl who likes to relax and be alone sometimes. A girl who wants to make the world a better place, a child who wants to talk to animals, a girl who wants to grow wings. A tiny star in the universe, a girl who loves to dream. A person who doesn't mind jagged edges, a person who wants to see the whole world some day. A girl who likes to wish on stars and let her shadow lead the way. A girl who wants to stand on her head to see the world from a different angle, a girl who never wants to see the future, but wants everything to be a great big guessing game."

The person who wrote this is someone I've known for many years. I've seen her run around until her eyes water from the wind. I've watched her perform in school concerts. I've seen her work with other kids in the library. But I never guessed the lengths to which she's been exploring, experiencing, and wondering about her world.

I found another student's short essay. This person wrote in a direct style that made me think of the many challenges that kids face every day in growing up. She wrote, "I feel like the world is moving so fast that I can barely keep up. I want to have a good life with all that I can have. I want to ignore everyone who says that I can't do something. I believe that nobody is stupid or weird, but that everyone is special. I want to see a lot of the world. I am just a 12-year-old girl but my thoughts really do matter. I have my dreams, and I hope they will come true."

It would be hard to find more eloquent statements of kids' dreams and aspirations. Kids who were just figures at the bus stop appeared in completely different dimensions. I had been missing that these weren't simply last year's kids with a few inches of growth and a new backpack to mark the passage of time. They were young adults who were discovering that the world was much bigger than the town where they were growing up. They were young adults wondering how they will fit into this world. They already carried in their minds many of the hopes and fears, aspirations, and apprehensions that adults bear as we go through life.

So, please. Make a new year's resolution now. Next school year, each one of us will spend a couple of hours in our children's schools—at an art show, at a concert, at a science fair, at a math night, maybe even in a class. And this is a resolution not just for parents, but for all adults in our communities. We've got to connect with kids, and I can think of no better way than hanging out where they hang out—at school.

PROFILES IN COURAGE

WHEN I WAS A KID, I was fascinated by the stories in John F. Kennedy's book *Profiles in Courage*. The point of the stories was that sometimes an elected official must listen not to the noise of the crowd but to the voice from his or her soul. You may not get reelected the next time you run for office, but you are at peace with yourself for doing the right thing.

To some extent, Kennedy's book was clever political marketing—a way for Kennedy to promote himself by memorializing others. The stories of forgotten heroes helped Kennedy to build a national reputation that propelled him to the presidency.

The popularity of the book speaks to the attraction that we Americans feel for principled leaders. It may not be clear when the leaders are alive that they are, indeed, heroes for bucking the tide. But the passage of time can elevate them to a status rare in American politics.

I believe that we have been watching heroes at the Vermont Statehouse in recent weeks. We have been privileged to see the very best that democracy can offer—freely elected representatives choosing principle over self-preservation

Of course I'm referring to the vote in the Vermont House on the civil union bill. Reading news stories, listening to reports of the activities, watching our representatives during the floor debate—if you followed any of these things, you know you were part of a special moment. Folks weren't talking about easy stuff such as budgets and taxes. They were grappling with their thoughts about an institution centuries older than nearly everything else they know; about people who they themselves may have denigrated at some point in their lives; about religious teachings that seem to justify prejudice. And they were grappling with the reality that because of the vote they were about to cast, they might not be back in their seats next year.

I have always been fascinated by what motivates some people to choose one path when the crowd is heading the other way. I believe that often, when issues of civil rights and human dignity are involved, closeness to oppression and rejection can be a determining factor. This closeness may be an intellectual understanding, or it may be a personal experience. In either case, possessing this closeness is admirable. It suggests that you are able to walk in someone else's shoes and see the world from their perspective.

Could the overwhelming support among women in the House for the civil union bill be due to discrimination—subtle or direct—that they may have faced in their own lives? The speech by the one black member of the House alluded to the pain of the outsider. The speech of the only openly gay member eloquently described the injustice of discrimination he has felt. Like the remarks made earlier at two public hearings, these speeches underscored the responsibility of the majority to guarantee the rights of a minority.

In the television show based on his book, John Kennedy intoned, "These stories of past courage can teach, they can offer hope, and they can provide inspiration. But they cannot provide courage itself. For this, each person must look into his own soul."

Two weeks ago we watched 150 people look to their souls for guidance. The majority found reason to support the civil union bill. The measure is now in the Senate. The words that I hope the senators will remember as they consider this bill are those of Rep. Marion Milne of Washington. She is a Republican from a rural district not known as a haven for liberals. She knew that her political future, and the future of many other House members, could hinge on this one vote. She didn't blink from doing what she felt was right. "If I am measured only by this one vote in my entire public life, I have served my constituents well by voting for this bill," she said.

That's a profile in courage.

THE FIRST 100

YOU ARE NOT ELIGIBLE to become a lawyer, the Manchester, Vermont native was told, because of "the disability imposed by your married condition."

So said the Illinois Supreme Court in 1870 when Myra Colby Bradwell applied for admission to the Illinois bar. She had already taken and passed, with honors, the Illinois Bar Exam. But the court said she couldn't practice law.

Of course, it wasn't just Myra Colby Bradwell's "disability" as a wife that prevented her from becoming a lawyer. It was the fact that she was a woman. Allowing her to become a lawyer would "open the floodgates" to women for "every civil office," including governors and sheriffs, the court said. That wouldn't do. Besides, women lawyers would distract the men in the courtroom, endangering trial procedures.

Myra Colby Bradwell appealed to the U.S. Supreme Court. She lost there, too.

It wasn't until 1890 that Illinois allowed the Vermont native to join the bar, making her the first woman lawyer in America.

It's hard to keep in perspective the progress that our society has made in breaking through walls of discrimination. Just think: It was only a little more than 100 years ago that the first woman practiced law in this country. And consider this: It was only in 1978 that the 100th woman was admitted to the Vermont bar. Even as late as 1981, women lawyers made up only one-tenth of the Vermont bar.

Nationally, women now make up about a quarter of the legal profession. The American Bar Association projects that within ten years, they'll make up one-half. Vermont is already inching toward that figure. Today, about a third of Vermont's lawyers are women.

Much of this progress has been made within the lifetime of anyone twenty or older. Indeed, reading the articles in a recent *Vermont Bar Journal* celebrating the first 100 Vermont women in law makes you feel that you've been a witness to important events, without realizing it.

Vermont Law School graduated twenty-nine women in 1981; now the figure is seventy. The state's first woman judge was appointed in 1984. Today, about a third of Vermont's judges are women.

Laurie LeClair, the editor of *Vermont Bar Journal*, writes, "Women who became attorneys when females in the profession were anomalies had to be bold and imaginative."

Attorney Patricia Benelli points out that, "For the First 100, law was not a career to choose lightly. Even in the 1960s and '70s, few high school guidance counselors and college career advisors suggested the possibility of a career in law—other than one as a legal secretary—to promising women. Women graduated from high school when the employment ads still read, 'Help wanted—male' and 'Help wanted—female.'"

Because the "first 100" blazed a trail, there is now a critical mass of women in the profession. It seems normal that a woman should aspire to practice law. Montpelier attorney Dorothy Helling notes that "Women now have other women readily available as mentors, in virtually every area of the practice of law."

Have women made a difference in how law is practiced? "Not

directly," says Ellen Maloney, who was the state's first female superior court judge. "The mere inclusion of women as lawyers and judges per se does not constitute change," Ms. Maloney feels. She continues: "Profound changes will come through a more complete utilization of the cooperative, communal values often held by both men and women but more often, historically, by women."

Congratulations to Vermont's "first 100." They deserve our respect and thanks.

Vern Grubinger is the vegetable and berry specialist for the University of Vermont Extension Service, and the Director of the UVM Center for Sustainable Agriculture. He holds a Ph.D. in vegetable crops and an M.S. in agronomy from Cornell University, and a B.S. in plant and soil science from the University of Massachusetts. He has been writing silly stories on the side since third grade. (AUTHOR PHOTO BY TRACEY DEVLIN.)

THE FUTURE

THE YEAR IS 2051, and this is all things that *might* be considered, brought to you by NPR-NBC-CNN. President Ralph Nader, Jr., traveled to Europe today in an effort to revive stalled trade negotiations. The Europeans insist on maintaining their ban on all American imports in a last-ditch effort to salvage the remnants of their cultural heritage. The President is expected to offer funding to establish cultural museums, and to propose limiting exports of fast food and B movies.

The State of California and Archer Daniels Dow Chemical agreed to merge today, creating the largest public–private hybrid corporation ever formed under a new law that allows for the combining of commercial and government entities. The new state corporation will be called CaliDownia, Inc. A prepared statement declared this to be a victory for all citizens, because the new partnership will bypass bureaucratic oversight that hampers the productivity of our food and fiber system. The cost of lobbying lawmakers and conforming to state regulations will now be avoided, leading to significant savings that can be passed on to consumers.

The U.S. Department of Agribusiness today approved the commercial production of genetically engineered milk. A spokesrecording for the department said that the milk, produced by specialized microorganisms, has been thoroughly tested and is absolutely safe for human consumption. It's estimated that the new milk-producing technology will save dairy farmers hundreds of billions of dollars annually by avoiding the need for cows. The Food, Drug, and Recreational Supplements Administration has ruled that genetically engineered milk is substantially equivalent to regular milk, and therefore will not require any special labeling to distinguish it from milk that comes from outmoded animals.

In other agribusiness news, the deconstruction of shopping malls in the Midwest continues. Missouri and Iowa, now largely covered by parking lots, highways, and retail outlets, have embarked on an ambitious program to reclaim their once-great farming resource: soil. A multi-trillion-dollar fund has been established for the purchase of demolition rights at malls located on prime agricultural land. These malls are purchased at their agricultural use value, knocked down, and trucked to the Grand Canyon national landfill. The former mall sites are then made available to qualified farmers from Mexico, Cuba, and Brazil under the Farmer Immigration Act, designed to supplement the dangerously low number of remaining American farmers.

A strike by workers at Microsoft-AOL-Time-AT&T-Sony threatens to bring national electronic interfacing to a standstill. Monthly updates of office software, as required by law, are not taking place, and within the year many companies across the nation will have hopelessly obsolete communication networks. In an emergency measure, the Secretary of Communication Services has called for a temporary reactivation of the telephone system.

In local news, Vermont ski areas petitioned the Agency of Natural and Synthetic Resources for permission to cover an additional ten square miles of slopes in Teflon. Global warming has led to the conversion of all ski areas to grass-boarding, and it's become increasingly difficult to maintain live grass surfaces without natural rainfall. The Teflon coating not only avoids the need for water, but offers a faster ride without causing grass stains when you fall.

However, the impact of Teflon on wildlife is a slippery subject that may require further study.

In the legislature, Act 6000 continues to stir debate. The proposed legislation provides for statewide education funding based on a formula that calculates a town's annual expenditure on prescription drugs, divided by the number of civil unions it has performed, times the average annual sales of maple syrup. Opponents say that the law encourages consumption of sweets.

From NPR-CNN-NBC, in the year 2051, this has been all things that *might* be considered. Vern Grubinger reporting.

KINDERGARTEN WORM VISIT

EVERY YEAR, THE KINDERGARTEN at Guilford Central School invites me to visit with my traveling worms. These are composting worms, or red wigglers, that transform food and other organic wastes into crumbly black fertilizer. You can find them in old manure piles, or order them from gardening catalogs. Normally, I keep mine in a large wooden box at the office, where they dispose of a steady flow of coffee grounds, coffee filters, and lunch scraps. When it's time to take worms on a road trip, I shovel some into a plastic storage tub that's been punched with holes to let air in.

Visiting the kindergarten is like touring a model community. Everything that can be recycled is recycled, using color-coded bins for paper, glass, cardboard, and metal cans. There is a well-worn path to the outdoor compost pile. Every activity area is labeled with a colorful sign. The room is full of displays that show people's connection to the natural world. The idea of using worms to recycle wastes fits right in.

I arrive with my covered box, and the suspense is too much for the kids. They want it opened immediately so they can see the worms—the lecture on vermiculture can wait! I launch into my explanation of the ways and means of worm farming, and the tension builds.

I try to involve the squirming kids in a discussion of worm ecology. "What conditions do worms like?" I ask. "Dark," offers one child; "Wet," says another; "Dirty," says a third. Okay. "What do worms like to eat?" A boy raises his hand, digressing about his feelings for worms and the various things he and his brothers have done to worms. The teacher guides the class back on track and repeats the question. "Worms eat bugs," I'm told. "Well, not exactly," I respond, wondering whether to clarify the difference between insects and microbes. "They eat garbage," says another little voice. "That's right, some kinds of garbage—do they eat glass and metal?" A chorus of "no" rings out. "They eat things that come from plants," I suggest. "Like paper?" "Yes!" "And wood?" "If it's shredded up into small pieces they can handle, like sawdust." "And vegetables, too, don't they?" "Absolutely."

I explain that worms need some bedding to hang out in, a place they can go that is moist but not sloppy wet, with plenty of air. Shredded up newspaper, cardboard, or old leaves work well. Then a handful or two of food scraps can be added to the top of the bedding every day. Over time, they will eat up both the bedding and the food, producing worm castings. In a few months, the soil-like castings need to be removed. These can be put in the garden or in potted plants. Then fresh bedding has to be added to keep the worms happy.

"What happens to the worms when you take out the castings?" they want to know. "There is a way to keep most of them in the box," I assure them. "Because worms don't like bright light, you can take the lid off the box and they will move deep down into the castings, away from the light. Then you can skim off the top few inches of castings without removing the worms!"

Now the children are into it, and it's time to unveil the stars of the show. The small bodies crowd closely around me and peer into the dark box as I lift the lid. In the next few seconds, a hundred skinny red worms slither out of sight, diving away from the surface of the compost as soon as they sense the light. The kids excitedly share their thoughts: "Look, they're afraid." "Those worms aren't very big." "Can I touch one?"

I select a specimen, and it's passed from little hand to little hand, poked and rolled about to assure that it's really alive. "Is it a boy or a girl?" someone had to ask. "Well . . . , actually it's both." I glance at the teacher. Her eyes implore me, "Don't even go there . . ." Too late, I can't wiggle out of this one. "Worms are hermaphrodites, which means each one is a boy *and* a girl."

Now I'm looked at with suspicion: this worm guy is obviously not to be trusted. "Two worms get together, like a Mom and a Dad, then they *both* produce an egg—want to see some worm eggs?" There, I think I'm off the hook.

Fast as I can, I pick out a few lemon-shaped eggs the size of small peppercorns. These get passed around as I explain less confusing aspects of worm reproduction. "Several worms can hatch from each egg, which are really called cocoons. The baby worms look like little white threads when they're born." The littlest worms are too delicate to pass around, so I make my way around the circle so everybody gets a good look at the newborns. I think my credibility is restored.

Class is over, and I am given a recital of "thank-yous," and presented with a ribbon. It says, "To Dr. Worm from the Guilford kindergarten," and it's decorated with squiggly worms. Back at my office, I feel truly honored as I hang this recognition on my wall.

MUD SEASON

NORMALLY, I'M QUITE FOND of soil. I love the spongy feel of a silt loam underfoot when I visit a river-bottom vegetable farm, I relish the smell of freshly turned earth in my garden, and I can sense magic in that mix of minerals, microbes, air, and water that we so often take for granted. But for a few weeks each year, to me the soil is just dirt.

Those few weeks are called mud season, when the soil under fifty-four miles of unpaved road in my town turns to mush. To black-top dwellers, mud season is an amusing concept. But to my neighbors and me, it's serious business.

As our hillside wakes from winter's permafrost, the snow melts and the top few inches of ground thaw. The water can't percolate down through the frozen subsoil, so it blends with the solid part of our dirt road to form a colloidal suspension. That's what physicists call Jell-O. The resulting quagmire eats small cars and makes the task of getting to and from town more exciting than riding a roller coaster.

You need the right vehicle to travel the mud. Two-wheel drives get parked at the bottom of the hill when the mud demons are angriest. Four-wheel drives have a high survival rate if properly equipped. Forget about all-season tires labeled "mud and snow"— they aren't very good in either. Those who master the mud with ease ride on tires sporting raised white letters saying things like "Desert Commando," or "Speed King," which is odd, since the mud has nothing to do with either deserts or speed.

Technique is important, too. Even the best prepared will fail if their attention to the mud wanders, perhaps while listening to the radio, or enjoying the view of the woods as they drive. No, you must feel the mud as you go, stepping hard on the gas and heaving the steering wheel to and fro when it attempts to swallow you up.

My heart pounds when I leave the pavement and enter the mud zone. I look up the hill, scarred with ruts, some of them two feet deep, slick and shiny and ready to gobble up tires. I rev the engine, put it into gear, and charge upward. Rocking side to side, my tires spin as I slowly advance toward the safety of home, the soil splattering in the wheel wells loud and hard. Suddenly, there's a decrease in speed and it's the moment of truth. I grip the wheel tight and put the pedal to the metal. Stopping now would be surrender. Inch by inch I lurch forward until the treads grasp some solid matter, and I'm moving freely again. I exhale, and smile—I made it.

Next day, the temperatures have plummeted. The road is like a frozen railroad track after an earthquake. Gullies and hills as solid as icebergs await, ready to rip the undersides from cars that show too little respect. I drive a careful path, bumping and bouncing down the hill, straining to look ahead, fearing a really deep rut will take me wherever it likes.

Speed is the enemy now. Go too fast, and you'll be slammed around like a pinball. Too slow, and you won't get to work till noon. If there's delicate cargo on board, and you're in a rush, it's a bummer. I'll never forget the time I had my very pregnant wife in the pickup, and we were late for an appointment. The ruts were frozen and unforgiving. I hate being late, but I didn't want to deliver the baby on the way. Even at twenty miles an hour her belly heaved mightily about, almost independent of the rest of her. She smiled, I clenched my jaw. At long last we reached the bottom of the hill, still a family of two.

It makes me smile when city friends visit and ask, as they always do, "How's the road in winter?" referring, of course, to snow. "Oh, the town has it plowed and sanded by seven A.M. after every storm. It's the mud that we worry about." They look at me quizzically. "Come back and visit next spring," I tell them. "You'll see."

Cheryl Hanna is known for her commentary on the law and its place in Vermont life, but more generally she writes and speaks extensively on women, girls, violence, and social policy. A Harvard Law graduate, Cheryl served as an assistant district attorney in Baltimore City and is currently a professor of law at Vermont Law School. Her many and varied awards include the distinguished Margaret R. Williams Award from the Vermont Women in High Education, given to the outstanding emerging professional of the year, and the Irving R. Kaufman Fellowship from Harvard Law School.

When she isn't working, Cheryl enjoys watching movies and television, discovering new restaurants and wine, cooking, and traveling. She is currently forcing herself to learn to play golf. If she ever gets any good at the game, it will be the only sport she's ever mastered.

But she is not hopeful. (AUTHOR PHOTO BY BARBARA LESLIE.)

A MATTER OF TIME

I HAVE NO IDEA what possessed me to call Peter. We met while college students during our foreign study and eventually shared an apartment in London, just off Covent Garden. A perfect setting to be young, idealistic, and in love, albeit in that twenties sort of way.

It had been twelve years. After that "I can't believe it—how are you?" conversation, we agreed to meet again one day. And a few weeks ago, we did.

But before we did, I found my journal. The entry from just after we met reads: "October 17, 1986—On the train to Brugge to meet Peter. . . . The one thing that I want to feel when I die is that I never missed anything. Peter feels the same way, I think, and I want him to experience everything he can. Maybe we will meet at the turn of the century, and stay up all night drinking coffee and smoking cigarettes, and telling each other of all the places and people and desires that we have discovered."

Now, I have always believed in destiny—but after reading my journal, I knew it was only a matter of time.

He looked exactly the same—handsome, brave, and clouded in darkness—the kind of darkness that seems so cool in your twenties, and so rare in your thirties. And when I saw that James Dean poster that I had given him hanging in his home, my heart beat just a little bit faster.

After only a few minutes in the restaurant, well, it was as if no time had passed at all. He started to apologize for all the pain that he had caused me, but before I could tell him not to be sorry, that I knew all along, we were interrupted:

"A rose for the beautiful lady?"

"Not tonight," said Peter. "The husband is at home." The rose-seller raised her eyebrows. We laughed. It is Peter's husband who was at home, mind you, not mine. And all I can say is, better him than me.

You see, years after our inevitable breakup, Peter fell in love and married, not legally, of course. Marriage between same-sex partners is still not legally recognized, but I was definitely having dinner with a married man. Peter is remodeling their co-op and navigating two careers—he is stable and settled and domestic and committed—everything that back in London I thought that I should be, but wasn't.

I now live a too-busy-shattering-glass-ceilings-to-get-remarried–Marlo-Thomas-"That-Girl" kinda life. We agreed: no trading places. We love our lives as they are—not as we once wished them to be. Peter remarked that it just took time for both of us to "come out." I couldn't have said it better.

It's painful to accept that not everyone lives or loves the way in which you do. But it's when you feel that intense pain that you also feel truly alive, and brave, and a better person for it. Twelve years ago, I thought I would never recover from my broken heart, but it was only a matter of time.

To be honest, today, nothing would make me happier than to stand next to Peter at the altar during his legal marriage, not as his bride, but as his "best woman" as it were. And that too may only be a matter of time. Any day now, the Vermont Supreme Court will decide whether to legalize same-sex marriage. I hope that the justices will be brave and make the right call. After all, there's no better legacy for a lawyer than to be a leader—in love.

This is Cheryl Hanna—and I have no regrets.

BLACK ICE AND WHITE KNIGHTS

Vermont's Good Samaritan Law

ONE BEAUTIFUL, SUNNY SATURDAY, I was driving north on 89, just singing along to the latest pop hits, when my car started to skid. Black ice. My car spun around 180 degrees and smashed into the guard rail. I was facing the oncoming traffic. Somehow, I drove across two lanes into the breakdown lane. Just as I started to breathe a sigh of relief, another car traveling behind me hit the same patch of black ice, crashed into the guard rail, smashed my driver's side, bounced off the guard rail, and then, believe it or not, hit me again. I couldn't move.

But I could see something approaching in the rear view mirror—a black pickup truck. God must want me dead, I thought, and he is going to keep trying until he gets it right. I braced myself for the final and fatal blow. But the truck didn't hit me.

It stopped.

"You wouldn't happen to be the angel of death," I said to the driver as he helped me out of my car.

"Nope," he said. "Just a good Samaritan."

"You are an angel," I told him. "You didn't have to stop."

Actually, under Vermont Law, he did.

Vermont was the first state in the nation, and is one of only three, to have a Good Samaritan law. Translated into English, the law says that if someone is in danger, you must help, unless you or someone else could get hurt in the process. And if you do a reasonably good job, you can't be sued. Granted, my Good Samaritan may have fit through the legal loophole, given that he put himself in danger by stopping on an icy road. But the law compels him at least to weigh the risks of stopping before driving on.

A little history: The law was not passed by a bunch of do-gooders in the state house. Nor was it passed in response to the highly publicized case of Kitty Genovese, the New York woman who was stabbed to death while neighbors ignored her cries for help. It was passed to protect doctors. Medical professionals worried that if they rendered aid to a stranger in need, some lawyer would later sue. So, the legislature said no lawsuits, but that everyone, not only those who wear white coats, has a duty to rescue.

While Vermont's Good Samaritan law has been on the books for thirty years, it has been getting a lot of attention recently as other states contemplate passing similar laws in response to the David Cash case. Last year, Cash, a Berkeley sophomore, watched a friend attack a seven-year-old girl in a bathroom in a Nevada casino. Cash said nothing and did nothing. Moments after he left, his friend molested and murdered the girl. Neither California nor Nevada could prosecute Cash since it isn't against the law to witness an assault and remain silent. In Vermont, Cash would be a criminal.

Granted, Cash wouldn't be in jail. The only punishment for violating our Good Samaritan law is a $100 fine—no worse than a speeding ticket. And there is no evidence that it is ever enforced. A ridiculous law, some say—after all, you can't legislate morality.

They're wrong. The Good Samaritan law matters.

I know that it wasn't the law that made my white knight in the black pickup truck stop. Most people in Vermont don't even know that the law exists—I didn't until after my accident, and I teach criminal law. But sometimes the law acts as a mirror. When we hold it up, it reflects who we are, and sometimes, who we want to be. We should be proud that the Good Samaritan law is part of our legal landscape. After all, this isn't California, and this isn't New York.

The problem with black ice is that you can't see it coming. But if any of you hit it this winter, chances are someone will stop to help. Vermont is full of angels. It has to be. It's on the books.

THE ENDANGERED SPECIES ACT
DOESN'T MATTER

GET THIS: THE FISH and Wildlife Service recently served subpoenas on some of America's most well-to-do socialites. They were told to surrender their shawls. Yes—shawls. The government is seizing accessories.

It gets better. These are no run-of-the-mill, softer-side-of-Sears shawls. They are called shahtooshes—which is Persian for King of Wool. The fabric is apparently lighter, warmer, and far more beautiful than even cashmere. And at $2,000 to $50,000 each, ounce for ounce these wraps are worth more than gold. They are totally to die for.

Most bought their shahtooshes at a charity auction with their credit cards, which is how the government identified those under investigation. Others bought them at Tupperware-like parties or from other women directly. They were never sold in stores.

Shahtooshes are made from the wool of Tibetan antelopes, which have been on the Endangered Species list since 1975. Under the Endangered Species Act, it is illegal to purchase or own anything manufactured from an animal on the list. Now, the socialites claim that they had no idea that antelopes are slaughtered by the thousands to make these shawls. They were told that the shahtooshes were made from the tiny, fine, chin hairs of wild goats. Tibetan nomads carefully picked the hairs from trees and bushes and then spun them into an exquisite fabric. Wow—now there is a believable story. But unless it can be proven that the buyer knows—for a fact—that shawls came from an endangered species, the buyer isn't subject to criminal penalties. All the fashion police can do is raid the closets.

Just like cocaine, counterfeit money, and other contraband, the shahtooshes will eventually be destroyed, which seems like such a waste. Why not give them to the homeless, for example?

Well, the idea behind the Endangered Species Act is to remove all contraband from commerce. If you give them to the homeless, they'll just turn around and sell them on the black market to some fashion addict. To save the antelopes from extinction there must be no profit in poaching whatsoever. But the highly publicized government crackdown seems to be backfiring.

Although many celebrities are cooperating with authorities, some of the rich and famous have vowed to fight for their shawls to the bitter end. Some refuse to turn them in, especially those given as gifts. Asking for them back, as one prominent socialite said, is being an "Indian giver."

Well now, that's one of the best politically incorrect reasons that I have heard for breaking the law in a long time. And wearing illegal garments just became even more attractive—people are risking incarceration to buy up every shahtoosh they can get their diamond-adorned hands on. And no one seems to be embarrassed by being profiled in *Vanity Fair* as a self-absorbed, insensitive slave to fashion. Hey, you know what they say, there is no such thing as bad publicity.

But here is my favorite part. The subpoena is now a status symbol. Everyone who is anyone received an invite to testify before the grand jury. And what does one wear to the social event of the season? I suggest elegant but simple: tortoise-shell shoes, ivory jewelry, and a fur coat. That will make a real fashion statement that the Endangered Species Act doesn't matter. After all, when you go to battle, you should always dress to kill.

Ron Krupp began gardening on an Eastern Kentucky hillside in 1965, when two friends came by with a mule and an apron full of seeds. In 1969, he apprenticed under Erling Anderson, a master organic/biodynamic gardener from Sweden at Hill & Dale Farm in Putney, Vermont. Ron went on to run his own small farm in Saxton's River, Vermont, and founded the Brattleboro Farmers' Market in the early 1970s.

In 1996, Ron began writing a gardening column for the Vermont Times. *His writing on gardening has multiplied ever since. In addition to Vermont Public Radio commentary, Ron is currently completing his own gardening text,* The Woodchuck's Guide to Gardening, *which follows the four seasons in northern New England.* (AUTHOR PHOTO BY MARILYN MADDISON.)

ROUTE 30

EVERY SPRING, I LIKE to make a pilgrimage to southern Vermont to visit my friend Richard Foye, who lives on the Marlboro Branch of the Rock River in South Newfane. I travel from my home on Shelburne Bay down Route 7 to Middlebury, where that lovely ribbon of highway called Route 30 begins.

When I arrive in Middlebury, I need to stop for gas. For some odd reason, I have a flashback to when I was a kid and the whole family piled into the big Chrysler on Sundays for an outing. We would start our journey at the gas station, where the attendant would invariably ask, "Fill it up with Ethyl?" This was confusing to me as my next-door neighbor was Ethel Waldman, and I couldn't for the life of me figure out why Ethel was in our gas tank. In those days, Ethyl was the name given for premium octane gasoline. No one mentioned the lead.

Nowadays, at the self-service station in Middlebury, there is a computerized message on the pump that reads, "Welcome to so and so. Come on in and have a fresh cup of coffee." So when I go in to pay for the gas, I'm a little surprised when they charge me for the cup of Joe. Go figure.

From Middlebury I head south down Route 30, along the Seth Warner Memorial Highway, through the beautiful, slightly rolling hills of the Champlain Valley. Dairy farms are abundant in this region of Addison County. The meadows are filled with green grass and the striking yellow of dandelions. When I look east, I see the Green Mountain Range, and to the west the Adirondacks are shrouded in mist. I come to the lovely village of Cornwall and then onto Whiting, the heart of the Champlain Valley.

The journey continues down Route 30 into Rutland County, past Crown Point Monument Road to the town of Sudbury. At this point the agricultural landscape begins to change as I enter the lake region of Vermont. First come the woods and hills and then Lake Hortonia, Echo Lake, and Beebe Pond. In the wet areas I can see and almost taste the green and yellow of marsh marigold or what some old-timers call woodchuck spinach.

On down the road is the town of Hubbardton and Lake Bomoseen; and soon the landscape changes again. I pass under Route 4 and come to Castleton Corners. After meandering through the small college town of Poultney, with its funky nondesigner shops, I arrive at Lake Catherine where summer homes cluster at the edge of the road. The landscape changes again as I enter the Mettawee River Valley with the numerous dairy farms and wide, flat, freshly plowed brown fields. Further along, the towns of Pawlet, East Rupert, and Danby are quaint and prosperous.

Soon the Green Mountain Range and Mount Equinox loom above the rich river valley. It isn't long before I enter Manchester, and I'm suddenly surrounded by logos of Merrill Lynch, Evelyn and Crabtree, and Armani. Then Route 30 turns east over the spine of the Green Mountains and drops down into the West River Valley where the skunk cabbage is out in style.

As my journey ends, I feel just a little like the early pioneers, who followed the trails of the Native Americans, who followed the trails of the deer, and I followed them all.

FANNY'S KITCHEN GARDEN

THE ETHAN ALLEN HOMESTEAD lies in the wide meadows, rolling hills and scenic curves of the Winooski River. It is part of the land known as the Intervale. More than 200 years ago, Fanny Allen, Ethan Allen's second wife, planted many "heirloom varieties" of vegetables and herbs in her family's homestead garden. Heirloom seeds were just about the only seeds to be planted in those days, handed down from one generation to the next.

Fanny came all the way from Manhattan to live on the Vermont frontier. She not only adapted well to her new and wild surroundings, she embraced them. She became a noted botanist, consulted by local farmers, and was part of an extensive network of gardeners in the New World who exchanged ideas, seeds, and seedlings with European colleagues. Fanny and her children also collected flower samples, documenting plant varieties along the Winooski or "Onion" River, as it's called. This was an impressive achievement, given how pressed life was on the frontier. Her kitchen garden served as a source for the vegetables, medicines, and culinary herbs that sustained the eleven people living in the tiny household.

Fanny also grew hops for beer and flax for linen clothing. Most of this work was done by the women and children. Hops grow well in the rich floodplain soils of the Intervale, being used not only for beer making but also to dye clothes.

I wonder what Fanny Allen would think of the loss of plant diversity and seed varieties in today's modern world. Heirloom gardening is a way to step back from the pervasive plant hybrids with which we are all too familiar. Sure, those hybrid cucumbers are straight, but wouldn't it be interesting to present to your table an Early Short Prickly, a West Indian Gherkin, or a Long Green Turkey cuke? Heirloom varieties represent choice and diversity in our gardening practices.

It's only in the last hundred years that thousands of vegetables have become rare and extinct. Some we know from the descriptions in early farm journals. The Jewett bean, known as "the fastest bean in New Hampshire," is lost forever. The heirloom gardener who includes a rare bean variety in his or her garden or cares for an old apple tree like Seek-no-further is participating in a worldwide effort to preserve plant resources.

Today, Fanny's garden lives. The Ethan Allen Homestead Trust, a museum and historic site, has recreated the kitchen garden. Researchers have used traditional garden design methods and plant varieties to take the garden back to 1787, when Fanny first planted it. As examples, just look at the Early Blood turnips, the Vermont Cranberry beans, the Connecticut Field pumpkins, and Bee Balm, an herb used to make a favorite drink of patriots after the Boston Tea Party.

At this time of the year, when the maple leaves rest on the forest floor and the great V formations of the honkers fly overhead, Fanny and her children would be busy storing apples and vegetables in the root cellar and drying herbs.

For more information on the Ethan Allen Homestead, call 865–4566.

THE CONFESSIONS OF A
FRUSTRATED GARDENER

AS FALL CLOSES ITS DOORS and winter approaches, let's look back upon the gardening season of 2000 and listen to the woes and delights of a common variety of gardener.

This is the story of Christina Root. Three years ago, she made the decision to take some time off to recover from having been "a frustrated gardener." Then last summer Christina had a change of heart. She decided to jump back into the fray at the Tommy Thompson Community Garden in the Intervale in Burlington, a place where she felt she could get away from the "urban-ness" of it all.

Christina's work as a college professor is very demanding, so her first challenge arrived with the beginning of the planting season. Her friends told her to "front-load" the garden. What they meant was to create raised beds with lots of compost and mulch. They said that once the initial work was done, Christina could just sit back and enjoy the fruits of her labor. I told Christina that while her friends may have been well intentioned, they were living in a dream world. Even "front-loaded" garden beds need regular maintenance, and that takes time and elbow grease, and there will always be weeds.

Christina was full of optimism when the gardening season began. She said, "You go down to the plot early in May and the possibilities seem limitless. Summer has arrived, and it's lovely. The soil is tilled, there are no weeds, and all is right. Unconsciously, you might be asking yourself, how can I blow it?"

By mid May, Christina planted her first seeds in the earth. By June, the weeds and bugs had arrived. Then she had to go away for a week. Christine said, "I was doing all right up until then but when I came back the potato beetles had infested the young potato plants. The leaves were being eaten up by these strange larvae-like creatures. My potato plants looked like a moonscape with those strange things on them that first were squishy and then turned into armored tanks.

"Something happened psychologically. I felt that they had won the battle, and it was very hard for me to kill them. You see, you have to crunch the buggers and I am not a cruncher. So I picked them off and threw them into a bucket of water and they just kept swimming around. My husband Don came down to the garden and emptied the bucket and stomped on them. He is more of a cruncher."

Christina felt as if the garden stopped being hers at the moment the potato beetles established their primacy. And then the weeds crowded in and grew with utter abandon. She says that she began to have the feeling that she had borrowed the land from the potato bugs; from the previous year's sunflowers, which had self-seeded; and from the weeds, especially the ones with the tiny white flowers called gallant soldiers.

Still Christina ends by saying, "Gardening is the most sublime activity to do alone. It's so peaceful that you can just sort of lose yourself in the activity, and we all need to do things where we don't have to think all the time."

Although Christina was a frustrated gardener last summer, she plans to continue to work the soil in her home garden and grow lots of flowers.

Willem Lange is sixty-five years old. He still has most of his hair and wits, but neither of his original knees. A child of deaf parents, Will first came to New England to prep school in 1950 as an alternative to reform school in his native New York State. During most of the time since, he has been collecting stories about the unique people and places in this surprisingly funny part of the world.

Will has worked as a ranch hand, Adirondack guide, preacher, construction laborer, bobsled-run announcer, assembly-line worker, cab driver, bookkeeper, bartender, Outward Bound instructor, and, since 1972, a building and remodeling contractor in Hanover, New Hampshire. In 1981, he began writing "A Yankee Notebook," short pieces for several New England newspapers. In 1993, Will took to the air on Vermont Public Radio. His career has continued to expand ever since; his stories are now featured in newspapers, on public television, and in audio tape form. He and Ida, his wife of forty-one years, live on a dead-end dirt road in Etna, New Hampshire. (AUTHOR PHOTO BY DAN HABIB — CONCORD MONITOR.)

NEW ENGLAND REELING

THE OTHER DAY, when it snowed so, I was lucky enough to be right in my shop in the basement, and didn't have to go anywhere. So I just hummed along down there, watching the snow stack up on the windows and slowly shut out the sky. Then, about ten o'clock, the radio station took a break, and we heard the grim news:

"New England is reeling under the impact of blizzard conditions and record cold temperatures!" panted the announcer, and he went on to describe how awful it was out there—trains and planes stuck or grounded, folks dropping like cluster flies, cars stranded, homes without power. Sounded like a disaster.

"Judast!" I thought, "I'd better get out and take a look at this." So I pulled on my shoepacs, tuque, and down jacket, called the dog, and ventured out into the williwaw.

For a disaster scene, the yard seemed strangely unruffled. Foot of new snow, maybe, more coming down, but fluffy. Pretty cold, too—'bout eight below. Not a bad day for New England in January. I opened the garage door, started up my truck, and headed down the driveway.

My truck's only two-wheel drive, but in that light snow it had its feet right on the ground. The main problem was seeing; the snow was coming up over the hood. But I had the wheels in old ruts, and we were as good as on rails. As we came around the corner at the foot of our hill, right where the driveway meets the road, I could see the town plow'd left a windrow about four feet high. Too late to stop, so I poured it on. Nothing coming as far as I could see.

"Hang on!" I said. There was a huge, white explosion, and we were in the middle of the plowed road, headed right toward the village.

Down't the post office, Jean was poking the last of the mail into the boxes. I peeked around the corner to see if she was reeling. Nope. Same over't the store: Frank was spreadin' mayonnaise on a ham-and-Swiss. He looked all right to me, but I thought I'd better check.

"Frank," I asked, "are you reelin' from the effects of this storm?"

He looked over his shoulder. "What 'n hell are you talking about?"

"Uh, nothin'. Just checkin'." I got a lunch pie and left. We made it back into the garage just fine. The dog stayed outside to reel around in the snow for a while; I reeled inside to give Mother her mail.

I don't know why the media do that to us. Maybe any story, no matter how overblown, is better'n none. But all these stupendous adjectives and verbs have the effect in the long run of numbin' us worse than the weather might.

For generations Yankees have asked each other, "How cold 'dyou have it t' your place this mornin'?" And there's no way you can improve on "thirty-four below" by shrieking about the wind chill. Most folks hereabouts can tell if the wind's blowing. This hysteria smacks of those notices the government makes stove manufacturers put on their products: "Warning—May be hot when in operation."

We folks whose regional delicacy is New England boiled dinner don't need any lessons in grim reality; we've got that up to here. No matter how bad they say it's going to be, we've all seen it worse one time or another. Besides, one reason a lot of us live here is that flourishing in this climate is such a good, moral thing to do. It's decadent to be warm all the time.

I like to look at those calendars with full-color pictures of New England and count the cost of beauty. A fly fisherman playing a trout beneath a covered bridge reminds me of mosquitoes and black flies. A snow-drifted country lane makes my cracked fingers throb. Budding trees remind me of having to take off my muddy shoes every time I step into the house. A flower garden—annual crops of rocks. Smoke rising from a chimney—hauling wood.

If you live here by choice, you pay your dues, take what you can get, and endure what you have to. It's well worth it.

Whenever I hear the weather person trumpeting dangerous wind chills, I remember being on a log job one morning years ago at 50 below. I looked up the mountain, and there was Harley Branch, one of our truck drivers, walking back down the road with his gear shift lever hanging from his mitten. "God, Harley!" I hollered. "You must be 'bout frozen!"

"You just wait'll I take this shiftin' lever in to the old man," he said. "Be right warm around here in a minute!"

CATO PASSES

CATO'S BOWLS WERE EMPTY in the morning, so I filled 'em. But at midafternoon he hadn't touched either one. Hmm. That wasn't routine. I wondered where he was.

He got his name because, like Inspector Clouseau's valet, Cato, he used to lurk in hiding when I came home, and pounce on my feet with a sudden, tigerlike rush. I played with him the same game that Clouseau played, and sneaked silently through the quiet rooms, ready to be terrified. Cats, though, can't stop the twitching of their tails when they're about to pounce. I'd see his sticking up from behind the arm of the sofa or the coffee table, and we'd pounce at each other.

He also had the irritating habit of sneaking into rooms that are usually closed and unheated, whenever anyone went into them. So whenever he was missing, I went through the house, opening doors to the attic, cellar, guest room, and all the closets. When I got the right one, there he was, waiting, with a little bubble of a meow.

This time, though, nothing. I found myself peeking into places he'd never been in the twelve years I'd known him. I went through the garage, and up the ladder to the loft, where he often spent winter nights. Nothing. I walked around the house, tchking with my tongue against my teeth. This time of the year, a snow-white cat is the easiest thing in the world to see. I spotted half a dozen pieces of birch bark and a piece of paper towel. But no Cato.

I went inside. But I couldn't sit still. Stupidly, I retraced all the possibilities I'd just exhausted.

The noose of an inevitable conclusion was tightening around the neck of all the optimistic scenarios I could muster. This had happened before. I've buried my share of pets, and found it a bitter job: the quiet body lying behind the growing hole; the laying in the earth; the regretful farewell and quick covering up; sitting beside the fresh earth, tasting metallic grief between my teeth.

Living on the edge of the woods as we do, we overlap other creatures' territories. The deer feed on the rhododendrons, bears tear down the bird feeders, owls hoot from the swamp, and the cries of coyotes echo around the hillsides at night. The woods seem peaceful and serene, but they're teeming with predators, from shrews to fishers and foxes. Nor was Cato an innocent little white house kitty; many the morning, on my way out for the paper, I almost stepped on one of his grisly little offerings.

Calling the dog, I started a big circle around the house. I could see almost everything between me and the yard. The dog cruised around me, as sheep dogs do.

"Where's the kitty cat?" I asked her. She walked away in a straight line. I followed.

I spotted him from thirty yards away, a blob of white against brown needles beneath a hemlock tree. There was no point in hurrying, but I couldn't help it. Fur was scattered in a six-foot circle, oak leaves spattered with blood. He'd been killed and half-eaten, his skin peeled back as if by a human hunter. I lifted his body, trying to recreate the scene. The dog sat a few feet away, watching.

I dug the hole and laid him in it; scratched one last time the spot on his spine just ahead of his tail; smoothed his fur—so long, buddy—and filled the hole. I brought two stones from the wall nearby and covered him against being dug up. Then I had to tell my wife.

His bowls are gone from the laundry, his hair from the living-room furniture. The little soprano snore is gone from under the bed. I can read without having my book pushed aside. Like a stream flowing around a rock, our lives have closed again, and it almost seems as if Cato never existed. But if he never had, there wouldn't now be this hole where he used to be, for almost a fifth of my life.

NORM, YOU'RE RUINING MY LIFE!

⁂

I'VE HEARD IT SAID that television is ruining our lives. I'm not sure that television is the only thing ruining our lives, so I've generally tried to remain above expressing such an opinion. But recently I have received incontrovertible proof of it, and have decided to air out the evidence.

Those of you who have read *archy and mehitabel,* a collection of poems written, without punctuation or capitalization, by a cockroach named archy back in the '20s, may remember his friend mehitabel. mehitabel is a cat of easy virtue who in an earlier life was Cleopatra. She shacks up temporarily in a discarded theater trunk with a rascally old tomcat, a retired actor, and between them they lament the passing of the good old days of their respective careers. The theater cat sums it up: mehitabel, he says, both our professions are being ruined by amateurs.

Which is just the way I've been feeling lately. The television is to blame; and if there's one guy who embodies the crime, it's Norm Abrams!

For almost thirty years, most of my life has been taken up with carpentry. I know all about joist hangers, lookouts, box headers, waney lumber, and even twinning sticks. I've watched plumbers plumb, electricians wire, sheetrockers plaster, painters paint, and tilers tile. And though I truly feel modest about what I know, after thirty years I must know something. Which is why it's such a shock to me when on a Friday evening Mother says casually, "Tomorrow I'd like you to build me a couple of bookcases for the living room. I've got the paint and the shelf supports. We've got company for dinner Sunday, and I'd like to get the books put away by then."

That's not possible, and I tell her so.

"Of course it is. Norm just made a couple of bookcases on PBS in about half an hour."

Norm! Norm is wreaking havoc in the lives of professional carpenters and cabinetmakers. Otherwise-rational television viewers, who admit that most of what they watch is fantasy, suspend their skepticism when Norm shows how to do something. They think it's real!

"Okay," he says, "today we're going to build a couple of bookcases." He walks over to the lumber rack, selects a few clear, flat boards, and plops them down onto the workbench, where a set of drawings lies handy to the hovering camera. In real life, I stand around while Mother sketches her idea. I make a list of materials, climb into my truck, and drive to the lumberyard, where I paw through piles of lumber looking for a few good boards. Time I get home, Norm's been gone for an hour, and I haven't even started.

"Okay," says Norm, "now we take these side boards over to the bandsaw and cut out the half-circles for the feet." Some pencil marks have appeared on his boards as if by magic. I climb the shop stairs, cross the yard, and dig my saber saw and dividers out of the truck. Every time he sands a board, drills holes, or clamps things together, you see him pick up the tool, start to use it, and then put it down.

Mother hollers down the cellar stairs. "You get those painted by ten o'clock, we'll break for tea." Painted? Has she forgotten the rabbets for the back and shelves? And the plugs to hide the screws? And sanding everything twice?

Actually, she has. This is the woman who stands up pieces of plywood inside a bookcase to support the shelves, so when you take out a couple of books, the whole thing implodes like a collapsing hotel. Who would holler down the stairs to Michelangelo, "Hey, Mike! You finish that Pietá by noon, there's some soup and toasted cheese sandwiches up here!"

The movie *Gettysburg* tries to show Pickett's Charge in real time. I wish Norm would do the same in his cheerful little TV show. Maybe the rest of us would get some respect. mehitabel was right: Amateurs are ruining our profession.

Ted Levin has devoted his life to capturing the wilderness, with a camera, in books for adults and for children, and on audiotape and CD for those who like to listen. His wildlife photography, exhibited in galleries at home and abroad, has appeared in National Wildlife, Attaché, Audubon, Vermont Life, *and many other magazines. A particularly amazing photo of a giant luna moth made the front page of* The New York Times *in 1998.*

Ted's books of nature writing include Backtracking: The Way of a Naturalist *(Chelsea Green, 1987);* Blood Brook *(Chelsea Green, 1992), of which Louise Erdrich wrote, "*Blood Brook *will enlarge any world, enrich any view . . . I love* Blood Brook*"; and* Everglades National Park, *a guide to one of the crown jewels of the American National Park system. Among another handful of books for children, Ted coauthored* Creepy Crawly Creatures *(National Geographic Books) with his late wife, Linny. He has worked as a National Park Service naturalist, a Bronx Zoo zoologist, and an ecotour guide.*

And Ted is not finished: Currently he is at work on Liquid Land: The Natural and Unnatural History of the Florida Everglades, *to be published by University of Georgia Press.* (AUTHOR PHOTO © FLYING SQUIRREL GRAPHICS [JOHN DOUGLAS].)

OF BIRDS AND BASEBALL

LONG AGO, ON AN AUGUST night in Yankee Stadium, while more than a dozen nighthawks trolled for insects, I realized that my favorite pastimes could be enjoyed simultaneously.

Watching baseball and watching birds require similar skills. Both employ patience and imagination, sometimes deep thought; both progress slowly, appear boring from a distance, but are punctuated by bursts of joyous activity; neither is hampered by time.

Of the thirty major-league stadiums, twenty-three border large bodies of water. An arachnologist estimates seven to eight million spiders hang their webs in the lights above Cincinnati's Riverfront Stadium. He figures the spiders are attracted by uncountable numbers of insects that rise from the fecund Ohio River. Several years ago, while the Reds hosted the Dodgers, I paid more attention to purple martins, the spiders' chief competitor for mayflies, than to the ballgame.

Fenway Park, the stadium I most often visit, sits close to the Charles River, which empties its freight into nearby Boston Harbor. Today, the wind blows off the Atlantic, steadily eastward at ten to fifteen knots. Patrons in the box seats along the third base line, already in shadow, grow steadily more uncomfortable in the gathering chill. The sky above Fenway fills with gulls—herring, greater black-backed, ring-billed, a few laughing gulls in breeding plumage, whose black bulbous heads look like tiny batting helmets. Casey, my underdressed, ten-year-old son, snuggles against me. During the final three innings of the ballgame he continues to cheer for the Indians, while I comb the frothy sky for birds, hoping to tease out a rare treat.

Birds are so much a part of the scene at Fenway that Joe Mooney, the long-time buildings and grounds superintendent, forecasts the weather at the ballpark by the presence or absence of gulls. When the wind whistles out of the west, gulls ride the breeze far offshore; then Fenway belongs to the reprobates of the urban bird world—starlings, house sparrows, pigeons. Today, gulls are everywhere, drifting like so many lazy fly balls.

My single game record for birds at a ballpark is fourteen species at Shea Stadium, set in June of 1990. The game had a highlight that missed ESPN's ten P.M. baseball wrap up. It went like this. No score. Two outs top of the second. Bases loaded. Mark Gardiner, the Expos' weak hitting pitcher, stepped to the plate to face the Mets' David Cone. Five pitches later, the count was full. The runners broke. As Cone started his delivery, twenty-six Canada geese crossed in front of the moon over the head of right fielder Darryl Strawberry, who was oblivious. Gardiner struck out and the geese disappeared into the darkness over Flushing Bay.

For me the rivalry between the Yankees and the Red Sox takes on another dimension. My single game record for birds at an American League ballpark is thirteen species shared by Yankee Stadium and Fenway Park. I once had a kestrel hover above the bleachers in South Bronx, like a left fielder camped under a fly ball. The bird was probably scanning for mice attracted to the same Lucullan feast of hotdogs and peanuts that arouses starlings. One September evening at Fenway, I spotted a merlin smoking toward Boston Harbor, like a Randy Johnson fastball. While watching the Red Sox, I've seen an osprey and a great blue heron, long, slender, and graceful, a DiMaggio among local birds; while watching the Yankees, a barn owl and a great egret.

Major-league ballparks, of course, are not the only place where birds and baseball converge. Twice last year, while I umped the bases at Casey's Little League game, a peregrine flew over the field in Post Mills. At another Little League field, on the Florida Keys, two pairs of burrowing owls nest in the outfield. Because the nosy birds stand outside their burrows, watching the action like frustrated pitching coaches, U.S. Fish and Wildlife officers roped off a portion of left field. Whenever a batted ball lands inside the rope, it is declared an "owl rule double."

It's the top of the seventh at Fenway. Casey's still shivering. One out. Boston is ahead two to nothing. A double-crested cormorant appears over left field, flies stiff-winged toward right field, as the Indians' Travis Fryman breaks for second on Omar Vizquel's bunt. I catch the bird, but miss the play.

To fully appreciate birding and to fully appreciate baseball, you need a sense of mathematics and history, for both hold statistics and records in reverence. I leave the ballpark with eight species, far fewer than I had hoped to see. I'll be back when the weather warms, when birds and baseballs sail across a summer evening.

BIODIVERSITY AND PROPERTY RIGHTS

WHENEVER WE WATCH TELEVISION in our house, we almost always mute commercials. In fact, Casey and I often compete for the remote to see who can kill the sound first. But when I watched election results the other night, bouncing between CNN and PBS, I fell into an ad for the timber giant, Georgia Pacific. I wish I hadn't.

The commercial showed an angelic forester leading a group of children through an immaculate pine plantation, row after endless row of seedlings stretching to a stand of even-age pines. Unbridled monotony is what it was. At the commercial's end, looking directly at the children, the forester said, "Last year we planted eighty million trees, and for that I'm proud."

And for that I'm shocked. Eighty million trees probably covers more than 500 square miles of land. Five hundred square miles of now limited biodiversity. The simplicity of a pine plantation replaces the complicated and often convoluted interrelationships of a mature woodland, where hardwoods and softwoods compete for light and space and nutrients. Or worse, the plantation replaces an old-growth forest in the Pacific Northwest, where marbled murrelets nest 200 feet above the forest floor in trees that were here before Christ.

What's lost when a mega timber company like Georgia Pacific plants 500 square miles of parklike rows of trees? The living art of a woodland: the loss of the irreplaceable diversity of life whose ecologic and genetic information had been field tested and refined over millions of years. Comparing the number of species and the array of biologic functions between a tree plantation and a mature forest is like comparing Manilow to Mozart.

With very few exceptions, everywhere I look biodiversity is in retreat. The destruction of habitat, particularly in the tropics, where tree plantations replace rain forests, is one of the leading causes of local and regional extinctions in South America.

We live in an age of mass extinction. And the cause is us. A review of the fossil record shows that during the twentieth century the worldwide rate of mammal extinctions is one hundred times faster than at any period in the past seventy million years. For birds it's one thousand times faster. As we head toward the next millennium, no fewer than twenty-five percent of all mammal species and eleven percent of all bird species face possible extinction. No one keeps track of the loss of soil microbes whose shapeless shoulders support virtually every terrestrial ecosystem.

Harvard's Edward O. Wilson, preeminent authority on biodiversity, claims a conservative estimate of 27,000 species are doomed each year in the tropics. That's seventy-four species a day. Three each hour. Because of human activity the present rate of extinction in the tropics has accelerated between 1,000 and 10,000 times, says Wilson.

To stop the hemorrhaging of biologic wealth, we must reinvent the way we think about our world.

This morning I looked across our fawn-colored wetland and thought how fortunate I am to be part of a community that includes blue flag iris and three-way sedge, and how fortunate I am to live in a state that values marshes and swamps. No matter where you set roots, it's a privilege to own land. Having money to buy land is one thing; having the heart to love it is another. Landowners ought to meet their neighbors—the marsh wren, the American bittern, the barred owl—and ought to insist that the vital functions of woodland or wetland continue during tenure.

Since 1844 six species of birds have become extinct in North America: great auk, Carolina parakeet, Labrador duck, passenger pigeon, ivory-billed woodpecker, and Bachman's warbler, last seen in the mid 1970s. The Eskimo curlew hangs by a thread. Vermont's last resident bald eagles nested near Lake Bomoseen in the 1940s.

Watching Georgia Pacific take pride in the transformation of a howling landscape into a manicured plantation, hearing political candidates demand property rights legislation, I'm glad Vermont has Act 250 to help steer us toward a sane ecological balance in our landscape.

A CASE AGAINST CATAMOUNTS

I WISH THERE WERE mountain lions in Vermont. How I'd love the hills to be haunted by a big cat padding unseen through a hemlock ravine and along the far end of a frozen lake. I could look at deer and just by the way they'd move I'd know that a lion was part of their reality. I could see the reflection of a truly untamed landscape in their eyes. The deer would be wilder, more skittish, less inclined to loiter in my front yard.

But alas, I know too much about the secret life of the catamount to hope that it still roams the Green Mountains.

Several years ago, I spent three weeks with field biologists in the steamy woods of South Florida. We were tracking radio-collared Florida panthers. The Florida panther and the eastern cougar (or catamount) are geographic races of the same species, the wide-ranging mountain lion. Although the swamps of Florida are far removed from my front yard in Thetford Center, the panther taught me that native catamounts are more myth than substance, the terrestrial equivalent of Champ, a beast more suited to the realms of cryptozoology.

My theory is based on several aspects of mountain lion natural history: visibility, biology, and genetics.

There are approximately eighty lions in Florida and no one sees them. In Vermont, I believe there are none and everyone sees them. Since 1996, there have been sixty-one catamount sightings reported to the Vermont Fish and Wildlife Department, including an ink-black cat in Hartland that was supposed to be larger than a great Dane. Mountain lions, no matter where they live, match the color of deer, their principal food: a uniform fawn brown, a reddish brown, or a tawny brown on top, lighter below. Darrell Land, the lead biologist on the Florida Panther Recovery Team, told me that in fifteen years of field research he had only seen one animal in the wild without the aid of specially trained dogs—whose sole mission in life is to tree big cats—or high-tech equipment such as radio collars, satellite tracking systems, and low-flying airplanes. A radio-collared panther once spent three days hunkered down in a palmetto patch near an elementary school and a busy intersection in suburban Naples. No one saw it.

Last January I waited for several hours on a swamp buggy as a pair of camouflaged panthers interrupted their lovemaking and froze in place less than fifty feet away from me. I heard the beep, beep, beeping of their radio transmitters, but never saw the animals themselves.

What about the 1994 sighting of catamounts in Craftsbury, you might ask me? A U.S. Fish and Wildlife Laboratory confirmed that hairs found in the animals' scat were indeed cougar. But what kind of cougar were they? In the last couple of years there have been several big cats killed in the Northeast. DNA testing revealed that a six-month-old mountain lion recently shot in the Adirondacks belonged to a South American race. Another on the Ontario–Quebec border was of Chilean origin. Mountain lions are very easy to raise (I've done it myself), and the animals that occasionally turn up in the Northeast are most likely liberated pets.

Then there's the aspect of genetics. The Florida panther, which once ranged the coastal lowlands from central Texas east to South Carolina, and south to Florida, is now confined to portions of five counties centered around Big Cypress Swamp. Twenty-four panthers wear radio collars and bear names like Number 46. The genealogy of these particular cats is so well documented that Gregor Mendel would have been impressed.

In fact, Florida panthers and Mendel's garden peas have something in common. Both have limited genetic diversity. For peas, this was the result of Mendel's experiments in selective breeding. For the panther it's the result of decades of unholy trysts—fathers mating with daughters, mothers with sons. When the number of animals in a population falls below a particular threshold (unique to each species), inbreeding becomes unavoidable, which is a prescription for extinction. Male Florida panthers are born with only one testicle, have low sperm counts, holes in their hearts, leaky heart valves, and are sometimes fatally aggressive toward females.

Both sexes show signs of a collapsing immune system, the feline equivalent of AIDS.

Which brings me back to the catamount. In order to have them in Vermont (and across northern New England and the Adirondacks), we need a viable breeding population, not an individual or two or three. We need two hundred and fifty catamounts or more to maintain a healthy gene pool and tens of thousands of square miles of wild country to support them.

There is a houndsman in southwest Texas named Roy McBride, who makes his living treeing cats all over the world, both for research and for big game hunters. Since 1971, McBride and his sons have treed panthers for the state of Florida. A cat is a cat, McBride once told me. It doesn't matter whether it's in Vermont or Texas or Florida. They behave the same way.

Why don't we pass the hat and hire Roy McBride to settle the question in Vermont? He could tell us once and for all if catamounts prowl the Green Mountains. If he treed a big cat, a blood test would confirm its racial identity. And if there aren't catamounts around, why don't we bring them back? The heavily forested, deer-bloated Northeast offers plenty of food and good cover. As a matter of fact, I'd like one released in my front yard, close to the garden.

John McClaughry, a VPR commentator since 1993, is president of Vermont's free-market Ethan Allen Institute. Previously a member of the Vermont House and Senate, and senior policy advisor in the White House, John has also been Kirby's town moderator since 1967.
(AUTHOR PHOTO BY BARRY HAYES.)

SHARP PRACTICE

OVER THE PAST 220 YEARS the Vermont General Assembly, like any democratically elected legislative body, has done some fine and memorable things, and some foolish and costly things. On no occasion that I know of, however, had our legislators done something truly dishonorable. That, alas, has just changed.

At issue is a bill to change the legal rules of the Vermont court system. The purpose of the bill is to guarantee that one particular plaintiff—the state of Vermont—will be able to go into its own courts and extract at least $25 million from one particular group of defendants, Big Tobacco.

Now, one can make a credible case that the tobacco industry has done the world a lot of damage, and ought to be held to account for it. But what Attorney General William Sorrell got an ethically challenged General Assembly to do goes far beyond authorizing a tort lawsuit against Big Tobacco. Sorrell's bill declares that "affirmative defenses normally available to a defendant are abrogated to ensure full recovery." Sorrell's idea of justice is to rig the case in advance so he can't lose.

Sorrell's bill would allow the state to bring a case against Big

Tobacco not in the name of Medicaid patients with smoking-related afflictions, but in the name of the state itself. Further, the defendant's liability could be established by statistics, not by exhibiting individual victims. That is, if national studies show that, say, twelve percent of all Medicaid expenditures are smoking related, then Vermont could demand that the tobacco industry pay twelve percent of Vermont's Medicaid costs, year after year.

In hundreds of tort cases brought by individual smokers around the country, Big Tobacco has argued that the plaintiff knowingly assumed the risks of smoking and should be responsible for the health consequences. Juries almost always buy this argument. But Sorrell wants a sure thing, so his bill simply strips away the defenses and for all practical purposes declares the state the victor.

The genesis of Sorrell's tobacco cases is interesting. There is a group of tobacco tort lawyers, headed by Steve Berman of Seattle, Richard Scruggs of Mississippi, and Ron Motley of South Carolina, who have gone from state to state to sell their services on a contingency basis to attorneys general eager to pocket big bucks from the much-despised tobacco industry. These three and others appear as "special assistant attorneys general for the state of Vermont" in Sorrell's pending 1997 case declaring tobacco a public health hazard and seeking multimillion-dollar fines and damages. The same lawyers will undoubtedly appear on Sorrell's Medicaid recovery brief, which will be filed just as soon as Sorrell can get the legislature to change the rules to ensure a victory.

Out of thirty-nine states accepting the services of this legal SWAT team, only one—Maine—is paying legal fees on a straight hourly basis. In Vermont, these "special assistant attorneys general" handling the state's case will get up to fifteen percent of the multimillion-dollar award that Sorrell's bill makes virtually a sure thing, depending on how soon the defendants cave in and pay.

The bill is explicitly targeted only at Big Tobacco, today's least popular defendant. But once this racket becomes ethically acceptable, similar legislation will give the state a surefire legal hunting license, aimed at one industry after another wherever a lucrative recovery appears possible. The state could sue liquor companies for the costs of alcoholism—after explaining away the state's wholesale liquor monopoly. The state could sue Ben & Jerry's for peddling artery-clogging fifteen percent butterfat ice cream, purposely made as tasty as possible to encourage addiction among children.

Yes, a state legislature may change the rules in civil tort cases. It may even be that a legislature can change the rules on the eve of the state's filing its own lawsuit and get away with it, especially in a Vermont Supreme Court that has already held that your life belongs to the state. But earlier Vermonters with some sense of integrity about the conduct of public business would have a ready name for this sort of thing: *sharp practice.*

THE RISE OF THE NANNY STATE

GOVERNOR DEAN'S REQUEST to the 1999 legislature that it enact a mandatory seat-belt law marked another step toward the creation of what the British call the "Nanny State."

The Governor's proposal would give law enforcement officers the right to stop any car they choose and, if the occupants are not wearing seat-belts, issue a citation. Under current law, dating to 1993, seat-belt citations can be issued only if the officer stops the car for some other legitimate reason and obtains a conviction.

It was only a matter of time before Vermont's Great Nanny came back for a primary offense seat-belt law. Such a law is required by the philosophy of government that holds that people are ninnies who need nannies, and that the state is the most all-knowing and dependable Nanny. "We're talking about saving lives here," intoned the governor, justifying this latest rush to make everything mandatory that is not forbidden.

Examples of Nannyism in once-free Vermont are numerous and, alas, growing.

Back in 1991 both Houses in the legislature passed a bill legalizing Fourth of July sparklers. Governor Dean vetoed it. What if a child should get hurt?

In 1992 the friends of the Nanny State actually passed a bill, signed by the Great Nanny, that made it a $50 fine for every day that a Vermonter used a fluorescent bulb that the Nanny State had not certified as suitably energy efficient. Only with difficulty was a companion measure defeated that would have put the Great Nanny in charge of your shower head.

Two years later came Justice John Dooley's historic dictum in the motorcycle helmet case. He upheld the mandatory helmet law because bikers who don't wear helmets might incur injuries: "We see no constitutional barrier to legislation that requires preventive measures to minimize health care costs that are inevitably imposed on society." There you have it: Your life belongs to the Nanny State.

Take health care. The Great Nanny is determined that every Vermonter be herded into some kind of government-controlled managed care or government-run single-payer health plan, so the amount of care can be rationed by care rationers controlled by the Great Nanny. Why not let people own their own heath insurance, shop around for a healthy lifestyle discount (illegal in Vermont), and make their own decisions? The Great Nanny believes that the ninnies won't know what to do. What if somebody got sick?

Or education. Why not let parents choose the school that is the best for their kids, instead of having to send them to the school the Great Nanny thinks is best for them? Absolutely not (unless they are willing to pay tuition out of their own pockets). What if the parents should make a mistake and ruin their child? The Great Nanny is especially negative on parental choice because it would allow an escape from government-monopoly, union-controlled public schools thought by parents to be unresponsive to their child's needs.

"People are chumps," declare the friends of the Nanny State. "We are smart! We care deeply! We'll tell them what to do! And if they don't agree, we will give them a ticket, and they must pay for their insolence! The Nanny State is oh so compassionate, but it does *not* like to be crossed."

If the people of Vermont stand for the Nanny State's continuing invasions of their liberty, well, maybe the Nanny State is right: Maybe they are chumps.

VERMONT'S COMING
CRONY CAPITALISM

TEXTBOOK CAPITALISM IS an economic system in which the government establishes some basic rules, such as rights to property, enforcement of contracts, liability for damages, an independent judiciary to settle disputes, and a stable and predictable tax system. The government also provides a basic transportation infrastructure, backs a stable currency, and brings lawbreakers to justice.

Given these ground rules and public services, individuals and corporations invest their funds, produce goods and services, and offer them on the market. If consumers respond, producers earn a return on their investment. In such a system it doesn't matter who you know. The rules apply fairly and equally to all, and who succeeds and who fails is determined by the marketplace.

Now consider "crony capitalism," the traditional description for most noncommunist Third World economies (plus, one might argue, Arkansas and Louisiana). In such countries, the only way to have your business succeed is to become a crony of the political leadership, through family and social ties, bribes, kickbacks, and political support.

With the passage of the "economic progress act" of 1993, the "economic advancement incentives" of 1998, and the "downtowns bill" of 1998, all coupled with Act 250, Vermont is on the way to a unique Yankee brand of "crony capitalism." The difference between Vermont and, say, Brazil is that in Vermont, at least for now, state permission, assistance, and subsidies will be given out for high-minded public reasons, not for corrupt individual benefit. But the aspiring entrepreneur who has no interest in cozying up to Vermont's political leadership will have just as much success as his or her counterpart in Brazil.

The goal of the people who are bringing crony capitalism to

Vermont is to control economic activity "for the people." And here is how it works.

First, the barriers to new enterprise must be raised—raised so high that no one can afford the time and money to get over them without government support. Business taxes are a barrier, but not an insurmountable one. The real barrier is the state's Byzantine, costly, expert-intensive, arbitrary, and seemingly endless regulatory process.

This process features Act 250, wetlands rules, labor and industry rules, workmen's compensation rules, and many others. Not only is there a multitude of permits and rules to be complied with, but the enforcing bureaucrats often seem to feel little urgency about giving timely and definitive answers to applicants, even when the fate of a small business owner's enterprise is hanging in the balance.

Once the barriers have been raised to daunting levels, the friendly state offers assistance—provided the applicant does all the politically correct things. That assistance includes all sorts of tax exemptions, credits, and stabilization. Also available are pointed messages from "upstairs" to the regulatory bureaucracy that a project should go forward, or be stopped. Husky is the classic example of a major project that sailed through the process, because the governor created a high-level task force to see that it did. The proposed gas station at exit 9 of I-91 is the current example of the opposite; the governor has vowed that it will never be built.

But these benefits to business don't come without a price. The price is that the applicant must locate the business where the state wants it, hire Vermont residents, pay high wages, offer extensive benefits, use Vermont resources, comply with state plans, be receptive to union organizing, and "strengthen the quality of life." Making contributions to organizations that promote these goals couldn't hurt, either.

For most of the tax benefits the applicant must prove that he or she satisfies all these requirements to the "Vermont Economic Progress Council," nine appointees of the governor who serve at his pleasure and are not confirmed by the Senate. This device is only one step removed from Gov. Howard Dean's original 1993 proposal that anyone wishing to enjoy the benefits of the "economic progress" tax credits had to obtain the governor's personal approval.

Is this "crony capitalism"? Well, if you can't overcome the many barriers Vermont's tax and regulatory system impose without obtaining special government benefits and advantages, it's hard to see why it's not. And no matter how high-minded it may seem at first, the inevitable result of such a system is a corrupted pseudo-capitalism that will drive off the entrepreneurs who despise making political deals to ensure business success. It will encourage those most eager to get rich by making mutually profitable deals with these in power in the government.

At least Vermont's version is likely to be much less violent than Guatemala's.

John Morton has participated in six Winter Olympic Games as an athlete, a coach, and as the U.S. Biathlon team leader. He has attended scores of national championships, Biathlon World Cup competitions, and the World University Games.

After eleven years as Head Coach of Men's Skiing at Dartmouth College, John wrote Don't Look Back, *a comprehensive guide to cross-country ski racing. More recently, he published* A Medal of Honor, *a novel about the Winter Olympics, currently in development as a film. His articles on the outdoors have appeared in more than two dozen publications.*

When not writing, John designs cross-country ski trails; he's currently at work on projects in Maine, New Hampshire, Vermont, and Michigan. He will serve as Chief of Course for the biathlon events at the 2002 Olympics in Salt Lake City. (AUTHOR PHOTO BY KATHERINE HOWELL MORTON.)

THE TORCH

PERHAPS THE MOST SIGNIFICANT symbol of the Olympic Games is the Olympic flame. Although just one of several rituals that have become part of the opening ceremony, the lighting of the Olympic flame seems to capture our emotions like nothing else.

By the Calgary Winter Games in 1988, the coast-to-coast torch run had become a national event in itself. Eighty-nine days before the start of the competitions in Alberta, the Olympic flame arrived in Newfoundland and began an 18,000-kilometer journey through all the Canadian provinces. The torch was carried by 6,500 Canadians of all ages and from all walks of life. They transported the flame on foot, by snowmachine, on dogsled, and even by wheelchair. On February 13, more than 200,000 people jammed the streets of

Calgary to cheer the flame on to McMahon Stadium where 60,000 more endured bone-chilling cold to witness its arrival.

The torch was carried into the stadium by two of Calgary's former Olympic heroes, Alpine skier Ken Reed and speed skater Cathy Priestner. Holding the flame aloft between them, they circled the stadium and approached the stairs to the cauldron. Then, to everyone's surprise, they passed the heavy torch to twelve-year-old Robyn Perry, who represented the youth of the world. Smiling all the way, she bounded to the very top of the stadium, reached high above her head, and tipped the torch into the huge cauldron, as thousands of spectators roared their approval.

A day later, in the mountain village of Canmore, two hours west of Calgary, I was discouraged. The magic of the opening ceremony had given way to the frustrating realities of my job as U.S. biathlon team leader. A couple of our athletes were fighting the flu, the press had begun its relentless pursuit of our top performer, Josh Thompson, and there had been harsh words between two members of our coaching staff. The Games were not yet a day old, and already I was up to my ears in alligators.

Sensing my discouragement, U.S. Biathlon's executive director Jed Williamson suggested we take a break from the stress of the Athlete's Village by walking to downtown Canmore, about a mile away.

"Come on, John, they're supposed to be running the torch through town on its way up to the Nordic Center. If we get to Main Street in time, we might get a good look as it goes by."

With several problems confronting me, I reluctantly agreed to join Jed. As we approached Main Street we could see a throng lining the sidewalk. When we were close enough, we asked a bystander if the torch runners were approaching.

"They're already here," an enthusiastic woman responded, pulling us into the crowd for a better look.

I'll never know whether it was part of the plan, or if some magnanimous torchbearer simply wanted to include the townspeople in the pageantry, but the official Olympic torch was slowly making its way up Main Street, handed reverently from one spectator to the next. The brightly uniformed runners were walking beside the line of citizens, keeping pace with the torch's progress. There was no cheering or shouting; hundreds of people simply stood in quiet awe of the Olympic flame.

Jed and I remained where the woman had pulled us into the crowd, but as the torch approached, I was afraid we had unintentionally stumbled into a solemn ritual reserved for the host country, or perhaps just the residents of Canmore. When the Canadian woman sensed my concern, she said, "Stay put! You guys are on an Olympic team, for crying out loud."

Moments later the torch was handed to Jed. He looked into the golden flame as he turned, smiled, and held the torch out to me. It was heavy. I could smell the fuel oil, and feel its heat on my face. I tried to take in the detail of the intricate metalwork which held the flame, and the delicate carving on the wooden handle. In an instant, I was passing it on to the generous woman who had pulled us into the crowd.

It was a powerful moment. Even after six Winter Olympics, it is one of the experiences I remember most vividly. To actually hold the Olympic flame put me in touch with the magnificent history of the Games, and to pass the torch on . . . well, that's what the Olympics are really all about.

THE JOYS OF ROLLER SKIING

AFTER SERVING AS HEAD COACH of men's skiing at Dartmouth College for eleven years, I'd like to forget only a handful of incidents. Ironically, the most vivid of these doesn't even involve snow.

Roller skiing is the most specific form of off-season training for cross-country. Equipped with ski poles and stubby, wheeled slats, similar to inline skates, Nordic racers kick, glide, and skate the back roads of northern New England throughout the summer and fall.

One of the many traditions I inherited at Dartmouth was a fifty-kilometer, roller-ski time trial the Sunday before Thanksgiving. The event started on the Norwich town green and climbed through the hills to Union Village, Thetford, then finally back to Norwich. It was a tough, three-hour endurance test, and included some very fast descents, two with sharp turns into scenic covered bridges. I had severe misgivings about the safety of the route, especially for the younger athletes who lacked experience on roller skis. But the time trial was a well-established Dartmouth Ski Team tradition, a rite of passage for the freshmen, and I hesitated to undermine any sacred Dartmouth traditions in my rookie year as coach.

After starting the athletes at one-minute intervals, I drove the van along the route, providing water stations and encouragement. By the time I reached the common on Thetford Hill, there was a spread of thirty minutes between the faster and slower skiers.

As I approached a steep curve above the Union Village covered bridge, I thought I had overtaken everyone, but I couldn't be sure. As I hopped out of the van, my heart stopped. There was a ghastly smear of congealed blood across the road! I stared at the dark red stain in horror, visualizing one of my skiers plowing into the hood of an oncoming car; the panicked driver throwing the broken body into the back seat for a hopeless rush to the hospital.

At that instant, one of my athletes thundered around the corner. He was crouched low, legs spread, and skis vibrating wildly on the rough pavement. Sparks flew from his pole tips as he dragged them in a futile effort to slow down. His eyes widened in terror as he approached the steep, twisting descent to the quaint covered bridge.

I sprinted full-speed behind the skier and grabbed the waistband of his pants. As I slowed to a jog and then a walk, the color returned to his face. From a standing start, a hundred yards above the bridge, the turn was negotiable. I released my grip and watched him roll smoothly into the opening of the bridge. Then I sprinted back up the hill to intercept the next skier, sickened by the slippery smear of blood on the road.

One by one the athletes roared into sight. I raced to catch them, slowed them to a stop, released my grip, then bolted back up the hill.

Joe Cook, a local celebrity whose house guards the entrance to the bridge, found it so entertaining that he pulled a lawn chair to the edge of his porch and sat down to enjoy the show. As I labored up and down, Joe watched with the detached amusement of a world-class figure-skating judge.

When I was pretty sure everyone had passed the bloody corner, I jumped back in the van and pulled onto the pavement. But in the rearview mirror, I caught a glimpse of David Wilhauer, a freshman who had never roller skied before arriving at Dartmouth in September. He was hunched down in a bowlegged crouch and so petrified that he made not the slightest effort to reduce his speed. I slammed the van into Park as David shot past.

Scrambling from the seat, I lunged and grabbed in one desperate motion! I caught the elastic waistband and yanked him to a stop like the arresting cable on an aircraft carrier. He was shaking uncontrollably and couldn't talk. Trying to sound calm, I said, "Take your skis and poles off. I'll go get the van. You've had enough training for one day."

As I hiked up the hill for the last time, Joe Cook stood and began to clap.

"Sunafagun, that was great! You fellas gonna do this ev'ry Sunday mornin'?"

"No way," I responded, "this is the last time as long as I'm the coach." As a dreaded afterthought, I asked, "Was there an accident here earlier?"

"What?" Joe looked bewildered.

"All that blood on the road. Did one of my guys get hit?"

Joe's face resolved into a broad smile. "Oh that? Hell no. One 'a the Barker boys got hisself a nice little buck 'bout sunrise; had to drag it up the bank an 'crost the road ta 'is pickup. Thet's deer blood ya see there!"

COMPETITIVE GARDENING

IF THERE'S ONE THING an endurance athlete hates, it's quitting. At some point in every long race, the blisters, the frost-nipped fingers, or the overwhelming sense of fatigue makes dropping out seem like a very reasonable option. But every competitor knows that quitting once makes it easier to drop out the next time that things get tough. So endurance athletes resist giving up, at anything . . . ever!

For this reason, it's with a significant amount of shame that I'm forced to admit, I've given up gardening. I simply can't stand the competition.

Years ago, when we returned to Vermont from Alaska, I eagerly planted a massive vegetable garden. Growing vegetables in Alaska was for masochists. Oh, those postcards you've seen of seventy-pound cabbages from the Matanuska Valley, they're authentic, all right. Summer days with twenty hours of sunlight can do amazing things to some plants. But how many mouth-watering recipes do you know for cabbage or Brussels sprouts? Then of course, there were the moose. Those giant cabbages are just appetizers for a typical Alaskan moose, and what they don't eat, they trample.

So I was really fired up about gardening when we returned to Vermont, after ten years in the Land of the Midnight Sun. I roto-tilled half the open land on our property and spent fifty bucks on seeds. I hauled and spread several truckloads of cow manure. When the garden site was finally ready, I went wild. I planted three varieties of potatoes, four types of tomatoes, and five strains of sweet corn. I had pickling cucumbers and salad cucumbers. I started cantaloupe and watermelon. I had bib lettuce, leaf lettuce, and iceberg lettuce. I went way overboard with peas and beans. I got so excited, I planted stuff we didn't even eat, like beets and chard.

Having struggled with an Alaskan garden, I thought I was prepared for Mother Nature's challenges. I knew there would be days when I'd be engulfed by mosquitoes while I weeded. No doubt there would be dry spells, when I'd have to haul water until my hands hung below my knees. What I didn't anticipate was how methodically a woodchuck can clean off row after row of tender seedlings. I was amazed by how fast I cultivated a vast population of Colorado potato beetles. I learned firsthand about aphids, cutworms, and slugs.

But I fought hard against the bugs and worms because, miraculously, some of my seedlings were actually surviving! With great pride, I began to haul my home-grown delicacies to the kitchen for my wife and daughter. The first few zucchini were greeted with enthusiasm, but before long, it was suggested that I should share zucchini with the neighbors. People were polite at first, but one crusty old friend was more candid. "You beginning gardeners are all the same," he said. "I appreciate your generosity, but what am I going to do with forty pounds of zucchini? I have a garden of my own, you know."

About that time the broccoli started coming in, and in my eagerness to get it on the table, I made an unfortunate mistake. There are these perfectly camouflaged, pale green worms, which are hard to detect on the stalks of the plant. They're far more visible after they've been steamed with the vegetable. When my daughter discovered a couple of these delicacies on her plate, that was about it for garden-fresh produce, as far as she was concerned.

Then the deer moved in to help the woodchucks finish off anything that was still green. Although I was pretty discouraged, the promise of row after row of tall, healthy sweet corn kept me in the garden. But after almost three months of weeding, watering, and watching the five varieties of towering corn mature, the raccoons took over. In one night they did about as much damage as a D-8 bulldozer. They couldn't eat it all, but they took one good bite out of every ear!

In retrospect, I might have been able to face all the challenges Mother Nature threw at me: the weather, the bugs, and even the wild animals. It was actually my friends who forced me to give up gardening. Have you ever noticed how conversations in the summer eventually swing around to gardening; how many quarts of jam somebody made from their four strawberry plants, or how someone else picked fresh peas from their garden on Memorial Day, or how a friend just unearthed a Green Mountain potato that weighed four pounds? When I finally admitted to myself that I just couldn't compete, I quit. I'm still ashamed about it, but the summers are a lot less stressful.

Jules Older is a writer and the editor-in-chief of Ski Press *and* Ski Press USA, *North America's biggest ski and adventure magazines. His academic articles have appeared in leading medical and social science journals in five countries; his travel articles have been even more widely published, appearing in the* London, New York, Los Angeles *and* Washington Times, The Guardian *(London),* Hemispheres, *and* USAir Magazine, *among many other titles. His books for adults include* Touching Is Healing, Ski Vermont!, Cross-Country Skiing for Everyone, Backroad & Offroad Biking, *and* The Pakeha Papers. *Prominent among his twenty or more books for children is the 1997 title* Cow *(Charlesbridge Publishing), named a "Pick of the Lists" by the American Booksellers Association and a "Best Book" by Rathbone Children's Book Service.*

Jules has been a college counselor, psychology professor, medical educator, disc jockey, ski instructor, and, for one brief month of intense pleasure, a villain on television. In 1997, he won the University of Vermont's Kroepsch-Maurice Award for Excellence in Teaching for his most popular course, "Writing for Real." (AUTHOR PHOTO BY EFFIN OLDER.)

SEXUAL MADNESS

AS I SPEAK, our nation's media are in the midst of madness. There is talk—serious talk by serious commentators—of impeaching the President of the United States. There is talk of forced resignation, of inability to govern, of high crimes and misdemeanors.

Over what? A sexual encounter, real or imagined. Despite the President's denials, let us assume that it's real—when there's so much smoke from so many parts of the forest, fire is a reasonable assumption. And let us assume that it's just as tawdry and stupid as it appears—a nearly fifty-year-old man and a woman half his age;

he married, she young and flighty. And he having been down this road before, and now in the midst of a very public trial sponsored by his political enemies.

If true, very dumb, very insensitive—Gary Hart with a lobotomy. I think almost all of us can agree on that.

But here's where things get tricky. Is this grounds for a Constitutional crisis? For the forced resignation or even impeachment of a sitting president?

I say no, no, no. And in the next three minutes I hope to persuade you at least to consider that you are being led down an alley you'll later wish you had avoided. As they say in politics, let's look at the issues.

Issue Number One: Does sexual stupidity imply general stupidity; and its corollary, does sexual extremism imply general incompetence?

If we were in 1940 and were choosing leaders by their sexual discretion, Adolph Hitler might be an excellent candidate. As I recall, he showed little interest in sex. On the other hand, Oskar Schindler, the hero of *Schindler's List*, was described by his wife as "a compulsive adulterer."

Samuel Pepys, author of *Samuel Pepys Diary*, was a sexual adventurer of wild proportion—putting President Clinton deep in the shade. He was also one of the most important authors in England. And if you're about to argue that what's good for writers ain't good for statesmen, let me add that Pepys was also twice Secretary to the Admiralty, and is given full credit for building the strong British navy.

The list of effective statesmen and women with unconventional and unruly sex lives is long and distinguished. Unless you really prefer Richard Nixon to Jack Kennedy, I caution you: Don't confound sex and statesmanship.

Issue Two: What's going on here, anyway?

What I think is going on is this: In lands where sex is a great source of outer conflict and inner turmoil, e.g., us, people seem to go through periodic bursts of sexual madness. In the old days we expressed ourselves in this area by hanging witches on the gallows. Now that we are more civilized and sophisticated, we simply drive leaders from office.

Issue Three: Who's behind all this?

Well, in a way, we are, since we let it happen. And in a way, President Clinton is, since, like a yellow perch, he can't seem to stop himself from rising to the bait.

But if I were looking for the modern equivalent of the Inquisition, a latter-day Torquemada, in this tragic tale, I'd look no further than Kenneth Starr. This Republican operative and cigarette company hireling was appointed to investigate Whitewater. Remember Whitewater? A failed and shady real estate deal that went down when the Clintons were still back in Arkansas? Well, several years and many millions later, Starr is wiretapping, threatening, bullying, and intimidating a young woman about her sex life. His source? An older woman who has now denounced *two* sitting presidents for what she considers bad sex. Starr has gone from special counsel to grand inquisitor.

And friends, we—with a little help from the White House—are letting this happen.

Which brings me to my final issue: How come?

Well, let's look at how come the Republicans and the Democrats are so amazingly quiet on this question. It's generally attributed to confusion about what's the truth.

I think not. I attribute it to fear—fear that if they open their mouths, *their* sex lives will be the next subject for prime time exposure. Just as *I* fear that as you listen to this, you'll start wondering about *my* sex life.

You were just thinking about that? Funny, I was just wondering about yours. But what keeps either of us from looking too deeply into the subject is that we both know that this is a private affair—no matter how curious we are, it's none of our business. And I believe that the same good rule applies to the President of the United States.

APPROPRIATION

HERE'S HOW *The New York Times* reviewer Richard Eder described E. Annie Proulx's latest novel, *Close Range:* "She knows extraordinarily much about males: their bodies (who else writes of them with such lyrical respect?), the roughness and wary companionship of a raw macho society and a sporadic, startling sweetness."

I felt the same about Julian Barnes's description of the experience of a young girl in his novel *England, England.* It had a ring of truth as clear as a pure crystal goblet.

The world admires *Memoirs of a Geisha* by Arthur S. Golden and *Remains of the Day*, which is a search into the mind of a traditional English butler, by Kazuo Ishiguro.

So what? What's the point?

The point is that all these books would be banned, or at least derided, if the *appropriation* school of literary criticism had its way. For they all suffer from the same "flaw"—their main characters are not of the same gender and/or ethnicity as the author. The author is therefore "appropriating," an academic term for stealing or poaching into a province that is not his own.

I say "his" own because the finger of appropriation is most often aimed at males, and white males in particular. William Styron got it in spades for writing *The Confessions of Nat Turner.* In New Zealand, author Michael King caught it for writing on Maori leaders. I've caught a little appropriation flak, myself.

But even without that, I just hate the idea and the assumptions behind it. Why? Let me count the ways.

First, and I guess worst, is that the notion of literary appropriation strikes at the very heart of what fiction writers do. We make things up. We make people up. And the only limit we want applied to our characters is the limit of our imagination. I'm writing a book with three main characters: a Jewish boy from back East, a Montana boy in trouble with the law, and a black girl who's the catcher on a baseball team. If I took appropriation seriously, two of 'em would have to go.

Second, I firmly believe the world is a better place for "appropriation." If Annie Proulx hadn't written about Newfoundland because she was a Vermonter, *The Shipping News* would never have won all those awards. If Karen Hesse hadn't written about the Dust Bowl because *she's* a Vermonter, *Out of the Dust* would never have won *its* awards. Both books reveal the world, perhaps all the better because the authors viewed the place they were writing about with the fresh eyes of someone from away.

Third, if appropriation applies to writing, why not to other arts? Would the world be as rich, would women be better served, if Reubens didn't paint their likeness? If Picasso had limited his art to white European males? If Titian, if Rodin, if most of the visual artists of our millennium hadn't followed their own admiring vision?

Fourth, and for now, finally, when minority voices call for an end to appropriation of their culture, their stories, their heroes, they pose the greatest danger to . . . minority writers. Why should black artists be limited to black subjects? Jewish women to writing about Jewish women? Cree writing about Cree and not Sioux, Apache, or white settlers from Dalmatia?

My answer is that they shouldn't, that no writer should be limited by anything other than imagination.

ADVICE TO MY DAUGHTERS ON LEAVING FOR COLLEGE

THERE'S A TIME-HONORED TRADITION I'd like to revive. It's the tradition of a father giving advice to his son or daughter as they are about to leave home. As you're busy preparing for college, the time has come.

What I'm about to offer is only advice, not orders, instructions, or the One True Way. Here's a father's advice on sex, college, marriage, and raising children.

Sex

Sex is no sin, despite a myriad of preachings to the contrary. How do I know that I've got it right and the myriads have it wrong? Experience, intuition, and a lot of reading. Trust me on this one.

But if sex is no sin, neither is it, as other myriads would have it, just another natural function like eating and drinking. Sex is a lot more dangerous and thrilling than lunch.

College

College is one of those places you can get a good education—and where you can graduate without one. My advice is to get the diploma *and* the education. There's no extra charge.

Only it's hard to know what a good education consists of. I took advanced algebra and trigonometry and have never ever used either of them. On the other hand, I wasted a lot of time skiing and listening to rock and roll. Both have often come in handy, bringing me pleasure, subjects for writing, and a fair chunk of income.

The best things I did at college were as follows: becoming editor of the student newspaper, joining the ski club, joining the drama group, and auditing a course in modern art. Best of all was meeting your mother, which brings us to . . .

Marriage

Marry smart, by which I mean, marry for love. Love is real, all right; it's a real feeling whose presence—or absence—you should note well. Remember, if you marry with the intention of staying married (and I hope you will), you're going to be seeing that guy morning and night for an extraordinarily long time. Life will be a hell a lot more fun if you love him.

As for what used to worry me before I married—Shouldn't I be marrying "my own kind"?—this should prove no problem for you since you are such a rare kind. Really, how many half urban-Jewish, half farm-Protestant, half Yankee, half Kiwi writer-athletes are you going to find out there?

Raising Children

Although I know this subject is far from your thoughts at present, it may come in handy later.

You were raised with only two firm rules: no cigarettes and no motorcycles. We broke both rules when you got curious: I brought home a couple of cigarettes for you to puff on, and we let you drive the Morleys' little moped through the fields of Brownington. But these breaks were meant to strengthen the rules, and I think they did. You've made it thus far without incipient lung cancer or the after-effects of concussion.

So here's my advice: Make as few rules as you can, and more or less stick to them. Restrictions to build character or to assert your parental authority are usually a waste of time. I learned this lesson slowly; my teacher was your mother.

And, by the way, now that you are leaving home and approaching eighteen, I release you from the two rules you grew up with. I still hope you won't smoke or ride motorcycles or have unsmart sex or take dangerous drugs, and that you will wear a bicycle helmet and floss your teeth and all of that—but now it's for you to decide.

This is your loving father, Jules Older, in Albany, Vermont, the Soul of the Kingdom.

Ruth Page has a history of nurturing small ideas into vastly successful realities. Early in their marriage, Ruth and her husband bought a tab-sized Vermont weekly, The Suburban List; Ruth then began to edit and write editorials and features for the magazine. Eventually, The Suburban List won top awards from Harvard's Niemann Fellows in a New England-wide competition for weeklies. In 1979, she took over editorship of the National Gardening Association's monthly magazine, growing the circulation from a few thousand to over 250,000 nationally. And a half-time position writing and taping 5-minute gardening segments for radio eventually yielded an impressive national audience, brought together by over 170 public radio stations. In 1989, Houghton Mifflin published Ruth's gardener's bible, Ruth Page's Gardening Journal.*

In 1991, Ruth switched to weekly commentaries on the environment on Vermont Public Radio. One of the earliest voices of caution on now-common environmental issues like global warming, she continues to delight audiences today, and to combat threats to the natural world wherever she finds them.* (AUTHOR PHOTO BY SANDERS MILENS.)

COCKROACH

ENTOMOLOGIST HOWARD ENSIGN EVANS is an admirer of the cockroach, finds America roach-poor (we have only a few species), and pities us accordingly. The cockroach seems a contented creature with no worries about his fate. He has lived on earth for 250 million years, during which thousands of lovelier and larger species have been wiped out, so there seems no reason to believe a warming earth, or polluted air and water, or, of course, indignant women with brooms will affect his infinite adaptability.

While roaches are usually named for the countries they come from, on their endless tours around the world on rafts, in sailing vessels, and now in freighters, liners, planes, and anything else they can crawl aboard, this can be misleading. No country seems eager to claim one for its own, so a roach that originated in North Africa and then moved to Europe was called "Prussian" by the British, "British" by the Prussians, and "Russian" by the French.

Evans says in the United States we have the American, the German, the Oriental, and a couple of others. They are intelligent insects, having mastered mazes at a speed calculated to leave black beetles in the dust. However, you may be surprised to learn that the roach can learn some things even with his head cut off. He can live several days in this condition, his body "remembering" electric shocks and moving so as to avoid them.

If this behavior violates human reason, what of the roach's skunklike ability to spray enemies with a drug that gives them nervous seizures? He's not great at everything, though; it takes him from one to two hours to mate. His beauty doesn't attract females; he has to exude chemicals that taste so good she climbs on his back to eat them. He quickly does some fancy repositioning, so he can force her to stay with him. He hooks her to his body with a series of appendages that look like animated beer-can openers, a state of affairs for the female that elicits my sympathy. She clearly doesn't find him very interesting once the food's gone, probably preferring to head for the mall—hence his tight clutch. His relentless determination to continue the race, and especially his own genes, makes this admirable from a Darwinian standpoint.

Are you excited to learn there are 3,500 species of cockroaches? There's one (not here, luckily) that's four inches long. It has big horns behind its head and makes a loud hissing noise if you disturb it. Anyone silly enough to disturb a thing like that deserves whatever happens.

Cockroaches, it seems, are useful to humankind. They are handy in the laboratory: plentiful, easy to find and to keep, and have no laws or animal lovers trying to protect them. They can be used in basic studies of animal behavior, nutrition, and metabolism. They have even been useful in cancer research. Scientists have found that adding certain substances to the roach's body, or cutting certain nerves, causes tumors to develop. Study of such reactions can advance our understanding of cancer.

Roaches have an excellent early warning system. Not only do they have long and very busy antennae at the front, they have some shorter ones at the back called *cerci*, the Greek word for tails. The cerci are so sensitive to changes in the environment that if you merely blow on them, the roach will scurry away, a claim I don't plan to test. What would I say if someone picked that moment to visit? "It's okay, I'm just kneeling on the kitchen floor so I can blow on this cockroach's back end"?

There's one species in which the males tremble, raising ridges on their backs that rub against other ridges on their wings, making sounds that are not attractive to humans but appear to be music to that species's females. Both males and females of this species do the tremble-and-chirp act if you handle them. Researchers say the sounds are "protest cries." Uh-huh.

Roaches in the outdoor world hide their eggs, even digging a hole in the ground in which to "nest" them. In Florida, concerned roach moms tuck in the egg case after putting it in the ground, by exuding saliva that tamps sand down over it. In our houses, the females simply drop their egg packets on the floor wherever they happen to be, and hope for the best.

ROCK FOREST

HOW COULD IT HAVE TAKEN until the late 1980s to discover a whole forest no one had ever heard of before? Was it so new? So remote? Not at all. *International Wildlife* says it's the oldest intact forest ecosystem in eastern North America. It's along a cliff that runs for 460 miles through southern Ontario, then crosses the border and runs another 220 miles in Wisconsin. Huge, obvious, and right in our yard.

Of course people had seen these trees over the years, but they just looked like twisted green outgrowths on the Niagara escarpment, a 200-foot-high, white cliff: no big deal. Enter Douglas Larson, a botanist who spent years studying lichens, until a student gave him the dickens for wasting his life on those little scraps, when he could be studying trees that were able to survive on solid rock.

With Larson's backing, student Steve Spring headed for the rocks to examine the eastern white cedar, dominant cliff species. White cedars are usually described as species typical of lowlands, unlikely to live past the age of eighty. When Spring graduated, student Caedmon Nash went to the cliff to try to discover how much mass these cliffhangers accumulated in their precarious positions.

Spring and Larson hung on ropes over the cliff face and took long, slender borings from one typical gnarled, six-foot-long cedar, to check the tree's age. They couldn't see any growth rings in the pencil-thin core. But temperate-zone trees lay down a growth ring every year—what was wrong with this one? Back in the lab, Larson smoothed the surface of the core with a razor-sharp plane, hoping to make some rings visible. No luck. Then he started sanding the core with finer and finer pieces of sandpaper, until at last he could make out clear, tiny, tiny rings. Under a microscope, with the patience of a true researcher, he counted them. Unbelieving, he counted them three more times, until he couldn't deny the conclusion. That tree, only six feet high, ropy and twisted, was more than 400 years old. Larson said many of the rings were only two cells thick. It was Nature's own bonsai.

During that summer, student and prof examined 450 cedars. Trees born in the 1600s were common, and many first started life in the 1500s.

Of course when the news got out, Larson and Nash were hit with instant fame, at least in botanical circles, and some skepticism. Foresters were sure that if the trees were that old, they would have known it. Shaken, Larson hired dendrochronologist Peter Kelly to check his findings. The specialist verified Larson's work. In fact, he and a graduate student examined thirty-six sites along the length of the huge escarpment, and found ancient trees everywhere. The oldest cliff cedar on record, found by Kelly on an island in Lake Huron, lived to be 1,593 years old, yet attained a height of just twenty-five feet in that millennium and a half. On the entire escarpment, age distribution of the trees is appropriate for old-growth forests in the temperate zone.

So there you are—a whole "new" ancient forest that started around 500 A.D., and that no one had ever realized was there.

In 1987, a group called the Cliff Ecology Research Group, based in Larson's University of Guelph Botany Department, established a group of forty students to study the Niagara Escarpment. They discovered the cedars aren't living on the steep cliff because they like it there; they're living there because the abundant maples atop the cliff won't let them grow atop the cliff more than thirty feet from the cliff edge, so the rest grow on the cliff face. Maples apparently can't grow on the face.

Larson has established that the cedars are the slowest growing trees on record. When you see the sheer rock wall they're on, you're not surprised. How much nourishment could they get in such an environment? The researchers found one tree born about 1243, not long after the Crusades, that is only four inches high. Its diameter is a little greater than an American twenty-five-cent piece. A tree that was 155 years old weighed just half an ounce.

For centuries these marvelous old trees were ignored by humans, and that was their protection. Now, though, people know about them, so the trees face the usual threat. Tell people about something rare and unusual, and they want to get some and take it home. Road bikers and hikers have been removing the youngest trees, which are essential to keeping the ecosystem going. Ancient trees are declining, and even some of those are being collected as effortless bonsai to stick in a pot in the living room. Larson and others are trying to help the grabby public understand the value of preserving such an ancient, previously undisturbed ecosystem. In addition to its having earned our respect for sheer persistence, it can teach scientists about global warming, climate changes over the centuries, and may even offer some new medicinal sources.

ODORWORK

SOMETIMES SCIENTISTS SPEND MONEY to seek answers that any woman could provide, off the top of her head. Remember the astonishment of researchers some years ago when they discovered through experiments that in a matter of just a couple of weeks after birth, infants recognize their mothers' voices? Mothers have known that probably since our famous progenitor, Lucy, walked the African continent.

There have been numerous stories in the press reporting that researchers in Chicago have been checking to discover what aromas turn men on, neglecting to ask women first and save themselves hours of toil.

In one test the scientists fastened monitors to a group of male medical students, on their most intimate appendage, then had the men sniff odors such as roses, musk, Chanel No. 5, and a perfume called Obsession. Not one of these increased the blood flow in the male reaction site.

Of course, we women know what type of scent did start the blood flowing: It was the aroma of hot cinnamon buns fresh from the oven. It could as well have been lamb roasting, covered with onions and fresh thyme, or a smoking-hot deep-dish apple pie. Why else would we say the way to a man's heart is through his stomach?

Examining the power of scent to influence feelings and actions is a serious study, though it's only in recent years that considerable numbers of people have been looking into its mysteries. Several experiments have been underway. Some test whether pleasant odors soothe people in doctors' offices or in hospital rooms. (They do.)

What about people who have trouble falling asleep? Sound can help many of these—tapes of ocean waves, for example, or pleasant, slow music—so why not pleasant aromas?

One segment of the investigation tests whether the smell of delicious food can substitute for actually eating, and thus help an individual lose weight. Or could unpleasant odors take away all interest in eating? A neurologist taking part in the tests discovered that some folks who lose their sense of smell gain weight, up to as much as twenty pounds. That led him to test the power of scent on those who retain their sense of smell. When they had the scent of fresh corn chips to sniff, they lost weight. The more they sniffed, the more weight they lost. They averaged a loss of thirty pounds each in six months. Some of the folks sniffed almost constantly, losing even more.

Can aromas help you stay awake, or walk faster, or think more clearly? Many folks certainly think so. The aroma therapy business, which barely existed in the 1980s, was doing some $500 million a year by the late '90s.

There's a factory in Japan that releases lemon scent from its heating pipes to keep workers alert and productive. There's a professor in New York who keeps an air filter on his desktop to release the fragrance of citrus or peppermint, helping to keep himself and his students wide awake.

It's hard to guarantee the precision of some of these claims, and at least one researcher believes there's more fiction than fact in them. But persuasive information continues to appear. Chicago's Dr. Alan Hirsch insists that scent is vital in our lives. For example, he claims that "a large part of love (at first sight) is actually love at first sniff." He also says, "smell has the most powerful impact of any sense. . . . We have a whole universe at the tip of our noses that we do not even think about, that is virtually unexplored."

Some discoveries based on evidence from actual use of scent are these: People are more willing to buy Nike sneakers and will pay ten dollars more for them when trying them on in a floral-scented room. A Las Vegas casino tried scenting a slot machine area with a pleasant odor, and found gamblers shoved forty-five percent more quarters into those machines. And here's one I wish I'd known about in my school days: High school students in calculus class were connecting numbers in a maze. One group was asked to wear surgical masks that smelled sweetly of springtime; the control group breathed only the ambient classroom air. The aroma users worked three times as fast and three times as efficiently as the control group.

I know scent works powerfully on devoted gardeners. Watch them take deep, satisfying breaths when they enter a greenhouse in spring, where the rich aroma of fresh, moist earth and growing greenery encourages them to buy plants enough to equip a botanic garden. Like the folks buying Nike sneakers in sweet-smelling shoe shops, they are Aroma Activated.

Journalist, novelist, and nonfiction writer, Ron Powers is motivated by powerful, intertwining interests in American mass culture and in American "community"—particularly the ways in which mass culture and community influence and transform one another. This interest has produced a life's work both widely varied and highly celebrated. Prominent among his ten books are Flags of Our Fathers *(Bantam, 2000), a nonfiction collaboration with James Bradley, a son of one of the six flagraisers on Iwo Jima, which topped* The New York Times *bestseller list;* Dangerous Water: A Biography of the Boy Who Became Mark Twain *(Perseus, 1999), a study of the important Hannibal boyhood years of Samuel Langhorne Clemens; and* The Cruel Radiance *(University Press of New England), a collection of his writing including lectures on the craft of writing itself.*

Ron's television career has been equally impressive. The first TV critic to win the Pulitzer Prize in 1973, Ron went on to win both a Chicago Emmy and a National Emmy, this last for his work on CBS News Sunday Morning. *He has hosted programs on the Learning Channel and on Vermont Public Television. Ron and his wife, Honoree Fleming, have two sons, Dean Paul and Kevin.* (AUTHOR PHOTO BY MILLER PEARSALL.)

KIDS AND ENCHANTMENT

THE OTHER MORNING I went into my adolescent son's bedroom to shut off the clock radio that he'd left running when he hit the shower. I arrived just in time to hear the voice of a prototypical golden-throated studio announcer say something that those of you with strong Christian sensibilities will find painful to hear repeated. I am going to repeat it anyway, with apologies for that pain. I'm going to repeat it because I believe that only by paying close attention to such things can we understand exactly what is threatening the psychic health of our children in these anxious and volatile times.

This is what the announcer said: "And now, back to the Howard Stern show. For Christ's sake."

What if we have been asking the wrong questions all along? What if we have been using the wrong indicators to mark the assaults on the culture of childhood in America? What if the phrases and the labels and the categories we have used to identify forces that we fear are just a little bit beside the point? Not much, but just enough that the real evil, if you'll pardon that quaint term, is allowed to trickle through an unguarded entrance and have free play?

Among the phrases most yanked back into prominence after Littleton, Colorado, have been "violence" and "innocence." Violence, it keeps getting said, is on the increase in movies, television, and music aimed at children. And that violence has helped accelerate real violence, not to mention a wholesale loss of innocence.

The problem is that those arguments are all too easy to refute. Experts have a point when they respond that massacres at public schools remain extremely rare. A statistical speck. And as for innocence—haven't we been losing that since Kennedy was shot, if not since Eden? And isn't innocence, after all, an absence of something? How do you lose an absence, anyway?

But consider how the argument changes if you put these tired bromides back on the shelf and introduce some terms that have fresh meaning. Instead of "violence," for example, try thinking about "cynicism" and "anger." Not as easy to quantify on the bottom line—but it's well worth probing, I think, to assess the levels of these attitudes in the culture of kids; to trace their origins, and to study what kinds of behavior they are producing *short of* armed violence.

Which leads us directly to the concept of innocence. What if we put this unctuous phrase to rest and start talking about . . . enchantment? Amazement? The capacity to be inspired? Lifted up? Or to invoke another overworked but still-useful term . . . "transcendence." A possibility that is violated every time our kids are subjected to another jolt of mass-market cynicism such as, "And now, back to the Howard Stern show. For Christ's sake."

One of the best books about boyhood that I know is called *Boys Will Be Men*, written by Richard Hawley and published by Paul Eriksson here in Vermont. In it, Hawley argues that contrary to the pervasive stereotype, young boys do not set out to be base, profane, confrontational predators. They have always set out to be knights-errant—filled with wonder and adoration for the world and a desire to take their place in it as mature men. It is the world that redefines them as the sort of arrested, functionless creatures who snicker at the obscenities of Howard Stern. And seek transcendence in a syringe.

It is still possible for our society to help our children replace their present cynicism with enchantment. In fact, it's not just possible, it is our society's ancient and primary duty. But it won't happen until we identify the true obstacles for exactly who *we* are.

WOMEN'S FASHIONS

I AM HAVING MY morning cup of coffee in the window table of Calvi's ice cream shop in downtown Middlebury. There's a fly at the top of the page of the magazine I'm reading, Regis is cackling to Kathie Lee from the television up there beside the stuffed deer head on the wall, my bagel is chewy as warm taffy from the microwave oven, the morning sun is making my eyes water, and I am having a terrific time. I can't think of anyplace in the world where I would rather be.

I certainly would not want to be in the world that is depicted by the magazine in my hands. The magazine is *Vogue*. It is in fact the Fall Fashion Issue of *Vogue*, an edition that runs to 734 pages and weighs about four and a half pounds. Just now I am reading one of the articles about what women's fall fashions are going to be like. So is the fly, apparently; it's rubbing its little forelegs together in what looks like lubricious fascination.

What it says here is that women's fashions this fall are going to be hard and violent, because that's what femininity is all about in the '90s. What we're going to see is your basic S&M look: trashy thongs, spiky stilettos, patent straps, lots of skin-tight black leather, animal skins, and feathers. There's some other stuff, but it gets a little lurid. When the fly read it, it flew away. Maybe it was headed for New York, to be a fly on the wall.

So anyway, I'm reading this stuff, and I'm looking at the waitress behind the counter at Calvi's. She's maybe nineteen, right there in the *Vogue Magazine* high-fashion demographic, and she's pretty, but right now it looks as though spiky stilettos are the last thing on her mind. She's trying to do about five things at once: slice a bagel down the middle without cutting her fingers open, make change for the professor in a hurry with his bicycle parked outside, get a fresh pot of coffee going on the machine, answer the call of the slightly bewildered old woman who comes in there every morning, and through it all, try to catch what it is that's making Kathie Lee laugh so hard and so loud on the television beside the stuffed deer head.

"Women's fashions this fall are going to be hard and violent." I look at this kid. I don't know her; she's new here; and I wonder for a minute where she came from, where she might be going. There's another coffee shop up the street from here, across from the Civil War monument, and a while back they had a new waitress there, too: a pretty, utterly silent young woman with extremely long purple fingernails and purple bruises under her eyes. The fingernails may have been a fashion statement; the bruises were not. After a while she went away and we didn't see her anymore.

"Women's fashions this fall are going to be hard and violent." The waitress behind the counter is wearing blue jeans and a dark pullover that says "Calvi's" on the front. Where is she going? When she marries, maybe she'll be lucky and get a guy who isn't like *Vogue*'s idea of women's fashions. Hard and violent. Maybe she won't be so lucky. And then perhaps her future will include the hospital; the Addison County Parent-Child Center; Women in Crisis, her step-sister's spare bedroom; a court order.

"Women's fashions this fall are going to be hard and violent." No kidding. There are places around here where women's fashions every fall are hard and violent. It's a trend that *Vogue Magazine* might not have picked up on yet. *Vogue Magazine* is so out of touch.

THE YOUTH PROBLEM

I'M LOOKING AT THE local papers, and I can't find the word "youth" in a headline without finding the word "problem" attached to it, like a refrigerator magnet. "Youth Loitering Problem," it says here, and tells about a new law that makes it illegal. "Youth Smoking Problem"; they've got that one covered too. "Youth Dropout Problem." "Youth Skateboarding Problem." "Youth Problem Wearing Ugly Black Skintight Clothes Just Like We Did Forty Years Ago." (All right, I made that one up, but you get the point.)

You might think from all this that the children of America had been dropped here by flying saucers, instead of being conceived and reared by the rest of us. What are we going to do with these scary, grungy, sullen, tattooed, noisy green-haired aliens, these two-legged Problems who are spoiling the view and mucking up the balance sheet?

Let me tell you what one woman has done about it.

Her name is Colleen, and she's not a mother; she's not even married. She runs a lunch counter in the small town south of where I live.

Before she bought her little restaurant, Colleen used to manage a Burger King in a bigger town farther on down the road. This town was just big enough to have a population of kids who lived underneath the bridge, or inside junk cars, or ten to a flophouse apartment if they were rich. "Throwaway children," Colleen called them. She meant it ironically.

Colleen got to know these "throwaways" on winter nights. She had no choice. About forty of them would cluster around the drive-thru window where she was working. Colleen didn't get it for a while. Then she realized why it made sense. That was where all the heat escaped to the outside. "They'd be like hangin' around, hangin' around, hangin' around," she said. When Colleen also realized that the kids were starving, she would feed them the scraps of uneaten burgers and fries.

The problem kids appreciated that, but one gigantic Problem still remained. At about two o'clock in the morning, Colleen would have to put the cash from the day's receipts into a bag and take it to an all-night deposit box at the bank several blocks away. Not a fun trip when you're a woman in the night, outnumbered forty to one.

Colleen solved that problem. She didn't solve it by calling the cops or getting an antiloitering ordinance passed. She solved it by rounding up as many of these kids as she could cram into her pickup truck and letting them drive with her to the bank. Once there, she'd let one or two of them push the buttons that opened the glass door for the deposit.

"I never got mugged, never got robbed, never got threatened," she told me not long ago. "They had great loyalty to me. And I had no idea why."

I do. The kids were loyal to Colleen because she treated them like human beings, not like Problems. She fashioned them into a little community. And it worked. Is Colleen a "Do-Gooder," some kind of socialistical fuzzy-thinking liberal who doesn't have her head screwed on straight? No. She's a Vermonter. And what she did with the Problem kids was a little bit of Old Vermont, calling out to us from a past that is receding from us day by day. You take care of folks. You do what you can. Got a problem with that? I don't.

A regular and influential commentator for Vermont Public Radio and other radio programs, Olin Robison has written on public policy and international affairs for the last twenty-five years. His commentaries decode an increasingly complex world for American listeners and readers. Olin is the president of the Salzburg Seminar, based in Middlebury, Vermont. (AUTHOR PHOTO BY DENNIS O'BRIEN.)

THE TENTH ANNIVERSARY OF THE FALL OF THE WALL

NEXT TUESDAY, NOVEMBER 9, is the tenth anniversary of the fall of the Berlin Wall. It was on that date in 1989 that the truly unanticipated happened. The East German guards stood down; thousands upon thousands of people swarmed all over that twenty-eight-mile-long structure that, for more than a quarter of a century, divided not only East and West Berlin but in larger symbolic ways divided East and West, the free world from the communist world. The original Wall was put up overnight, August 12, 1961. The East German leadership called it their Antifascist Protective Barrier.

A persuasive argument can be made that the fall of the Wall was the seminal event of the late twentieth century. Indeed, it has been argued that it was the event that brought the twentieth century to a close and ushered in the twenty-first—never mind the upcoming celebrations to mark the advent of the year 2000.

It was one of those rare moments in history when everyone *knew* that we were all watching—and in some sense participating in—one of the most important events of modern history. We were all there that night in Berlin ten years ago.

It is also the case that ten years ago today [November 5, 1999] it was still not anticipated.

The truth is that no one saw it coming. There are now plenty of folks who claim to have predicted it, but that is mostly self-serving historical revisionism.

They—and we—were all taken by surprise. Neither Bush nor Gorbachev, nor the CIA, nor the KGB, nor the pundits in universities and think tanks—none of them predicted what happened.

Even Helmut Kohl, the West German Chancellor, was taken by surprise. If anyone should have anticipated this event, it was Kohl. West Germany, after all, had extraordinary intelligence assets deployed in East Germany. Yet Kohl, on November 9, 1989, was on a state visit to Poland.

Nor were there plans in the West about how to handle so momentous an event. As extraordinary as it now seems, there were no plans in Washington, London, or Paris for a reunited Germany. They simply did not exist.

The truth is that the West was rather hypocritical about German reunification, more than a little reluctant even to think about it. The broadly held position in Washington, London, and Paris was that each could publicly espouse German reunification without ever having to make good on it. The all too comfortable assumption was that the Soviets would never allow German reunification so there wasn't an issue.

One of the great foreign-policy successes of the Bush Administration was the speed with which it moved to facilitate the subsequent unification of the two Germanys. It was an exceptional example of agile diplomacy.

The fall of the Wall was, in many ways, the moment when world events shifted, if you will, to "fast-forward."

In less than *a year* the two Germanys became one again. In just over a year the entire Soviet system collapsed. In less than *two years* the Warsaw Pact was disbanded.

In 1989, the United Nations had one hundred and fifty-six members. Today, ten years later, that number is approaching two hundred.

The U.N. now even has a standing committee on the world map. It meets constantly.

What an extraordinary ten years it has been—the sort of period that lends substance to the idea that the old century has already ended and the new one is already well underway.

I have been repeatedly surprised, looking back, at the broadly held, usually unspoken, assumption that the fall of the Wall and the collapse of the communist order were inevitable, that they were predestined, that the only remarkable thing about them was the swiftness with which they happened.

It wasn't inevitable, of course. Certainly not in the short term.

Nor, was it inevitable that, when it came, there was so little violence. Remember, the Tiananmen Square massacre had been only five months before. In the weeks leading up to November 9, there was growing unrest all across the region and there were massive demonstrations. In Leipzig, for instance, the Monday evening public vigils had reached a point where literally hundreds of thousands of people came out and moved through the city with lighted candles—the crowd on one such evening was estimated at one million people.

The use of troops to put down these demonstrations in East Germany and elsewhere in Eastern Europe was not out of the question. It was a close call—one that went right for a change.

Not only did events go right for those people with all those candles, it was a time when events went right—no exaggeration— for the world.

What happened ten years ago made possible a brighter future for hundreds of millions of people. It also was the definitive moment in a process that brought to an end one of the darkest chapters in recent human history.

On the night of November 11, 1989, the Berlin Philharmonic played a celebratory concert on a makeshift stage set up at the Brandenburg Gate amid the rubble of the Wall. It played Beethoven. The huge crowd, hushed for the performance, went wild with enthusiasm. No one knows how many were there. But their cheers were heard 'round the world.

The CD of that concert, entitled simply *Das Konzert*, became the best selling classical CD in Europe for the next several years.

I get goose bumps every time I hear it.

TURKEY

THE DATE WAS DECEMBER 27, the year 537, the place, Constantinople. The occasion was the opening of the grand Byzantine Cathedral that came to be known as Aya Sophia. It had taken one thousand master craftsmen and ten thousand workers five years to build this extraordinary masterpiece, with its mosaic domes and grand multicolored marble pillars brought from the far reaches of the empire—from Boalbek, Heliopolis, Ephesus, and Delphi.

It is said that as the Emperor Justinian entered the cathedral side by side with the Grand Patriarch, the Emperor proclaimed his thanks for having the honor to construct so magnificent a church and excitedly shouted, "Solomon, I have surpassed you."

In this century, travelers on the Orient Express, the celebrated train that has long run from Paris to Istanbul, pass just below Aya Sophia, the great Blue Mosque, and the Topkapi Palace to arrive at the end of the line—the end of Europe. To continue eastward by train, one must take a ferry across the Bosphorus, and enter the other Istanbul train station, the one on the Asian side of the city.

It is a most exotic place with the unmistakable feel of the Middle East. Yet many Middle Easterners go there because to them it is European. It is both.

The hilly city rises on both sides of the Bosphorus, and the dominant feature is that most hilltops are crowned with domed mosques and surrounding minarets. In between are modern office and apartment complexes. Like Rome and Athens, it combines ancient and modern. But it is distinctive in its combination of East and West and has always considered itself the bridge between Europe and Asia.

Turkey is a secular Islamic society. Government and religion are genuinely distinct. But it is the only European country, unless you count Albania, where almost everyone is a Muslim. That makes most Western Europeans less than eager to see Turkey as a full member of the European Union. That is rarely the reason given, at least publicly. The nominally Christian Europeans are not yet comfortable with the idea of sixty million Muslims having full rights as Europeans, free to come and go as they please, to hold any job and have full representation in the European Parliament. Maybe later, but not yet.

Those sentiments did not, however, prevent Western Europeans from welcoming Turkey as an absolutely solid and dependable member of NATO. The Turks and the Russians have been enemies off and on for centuries, so it was natural that Turkey would have been a part of the alliance against the Soviet Union.

Turkish politics are not easily or quickly fathomed by outsiders. But this week is a good time to pay attention because what is happening there is of great importance to Europe, to the Middle East, to Central Asia, and to the United States.

Since 1993, the Prime Minister of Turkey has been Mrs. Tansu Ciller, an American-educated economist, who only entered politics in 1991. That a country whose population is ninety-nine percent Muslim should have a woman prime minister may seem an anomaly. But that possibility and reality are part of what differentiates Turkish politics from those of its neighbors to the east. This week Mrs. Ciller resigned.

She heads a minority political party that is considered center-right on the Turkish political spectrum. It can only govern if it forms a coalition with another minority party. This week the coalition fell apart.

She and her colleagues obviously hope they can hang on, forming a new government with her once more as prime minister. We'll see what happens.

The tension is between the centrists and those who would make Turkey more deliberately attentive to conservative Muslim demands.

Mrs. Ciller, who is very articulate and telegenic, has repeatedly pled for more European and American help and recognition for Turkey. Her argument is that what most Turks want is just that, acceptance by the West. It is the absence of that acceptance, according to her, which makes the Turkish political climate so uncertain.

Turkey's cherished self-image as the bridge between east and west is being put to an important test. Can it continue to be a genuinely multipartied democracy which also accommodates a conservative Islamic element?

A second, dramatically important, issue is that of making peace with a separatist-minded, sometimes violent, Kurdish minority against which the government has employed rather draconian measures. It is a dramatic and important time for an important country. If it can somehow meet these tests, then it will have bridged East and West in a most extraordinary and important way.

All the while, Istanbul sits astride the Bosphorus, that narrow channel through which all shipping passes between the Black Sea and the Mediterranean, between Russian, Ukrainian, and Central Asian oil and their world markets.

It has been strategically important from ancient times, long before Western Europe and North America had definition. It remains so today and clearly wants to play, once again, a part in bringing two of the world's disparate cultures together in a constructive and useful way.

GETTING BETTER RESULTS
FROM OUR EDUCATION SYSTEM

LAST WEEK AT THIS TIME I talked about the much-publicized results of the *Third International Mathematics and Science Study*, which were released late this spring, just before the end of the school year. In that study, involving students from many countries, American students were above average in math and science at the fourth-grade level, below average at the eighth-grade level, and at the absolute bottom at the twelfth-grade level.

I also made reference last week to the 1983 study entitled *A Nation At Risk*, which catalogued at great length a litany of woes afflicting American education. The summary statement presented to then-President Reagan and the American public stated, "If an unfriendly foreign power had attempted to impose on America the mediocre educational performance that exists today, we might have viewed it as an act of war."

And that was 15 years ago. I know of no one who would seriously argue that it has gotten any better. Most available evidence suggests that it has gotten worse. That would certainly appear to be the message of the *Third International Mathematics and Science Study*.

And so the big question is, how do we turn the trend around? First, a little history.

In the early days of the Republic it was not thought that the new nation actually needed all that many highly educated people. A few to teach, some to preach; a few judges and a few doctors. What the country needed was lots of people to do the hard physical labor of farming and of pushing back the wilderness.

In the twentieth century, and especially after World War II, that changed dramatically. A college degree replaced the high school diploma as the necessary ticket to a good job, and the numbers in America's colleges and universities practically exploded upward.

And then, in the 1960s, there was a subtle but dramatic change in public attitudes: Access to a college education ceased to be a privilege and, indeed, became an entitlement.

There has long existed a kind of paradox; on the one hand, education in America has always been seen as the road to self-betterment and improvement. It has been America's great secular religion. On the other hand, there has always been an underlying distrust of too much education, a rather vague suspicion that educators might take the nation's young people into some undesirable place of unsound values.

The values issues tend to get fought out at the local level. Sadly, these fights become diversionary, consuming great amounts of energy and causing much acrimony rather than building the broad consensus needed for strong schools. In such an environment, no one is satisfied, and paying for education is seen either as a burden or a luxury, when, in fact, it needs to be seen as an investment that pays off in a big way. It is an illusion to think that it can be had on the cheap.

Despite the acrimony and frustration, public opinion polls continue to show that there is a clear, unwavering public belief that education is *the* major foundation of the strength of the country. And there is a very strong public sentiment favoring a no-nonsense approach to the content of education. But there is little consensus as to what that means.

The public will support supplemental federal and state funding as long as control remains local. It has happened before.

After the launch of the Soviet Sputnik in the autumn of 1957, Congress enacted the National Defense Education Act of 1958. Billions and billions were invested in the educational system over the next generation.

The motivation was fear, but it achieved the desired results. All this, I might add, was largely under Republican leadership. President Eisenhower led the way.

It is time to do it again.

And, yes, that does mean more money. It is silly to think that the system can be radically improved without spending more. To claim otherwise is to lose sight of the goal. We therefore need a few political leaders, preferably Republicans, to call unabashedly for a great new, bold and imaginative *investment* in education.

The goal this time ought to be to create *incentives* rather than mandates. We ought to use tax dollars to give schools, teachers, and students incentives to excel in areas where there is a clear and present overriding need. For instance, twenty-eight percent of all high school math teachers and roughly half of all high school physics teachers have neither a college major nor minor in the fields in which they teach.

Money and incentives can change this.

So can scholarships. Why not create a new GI type bill for all high school graduates who achieve a certain proficiency in math and science? Is that in some sense discriminatory? Yes, it is. But it would be in response to a clear national need, and the public would applaud it if it were clear and focused.

And why not serious scholarships and even salaries for current high school teachers to return to university for a year?

It would take decades of aggressive spending before the total came anywhere close to the Savings and Loan bail out. Does *anyone* really think this is less important?

The name of the game is investment: creative investment, yes, investment in education. Especially in math and science. Why are we so timid? How much worse does it have to get?

Dan Rockmore, a professor of mathematics and computer science at Dartmouth College, may well be the only radio math commentator in the country. His mathematically inspired essays have been featured on NPR's "Sounds Like Science," as well as in the Dallas Morning News, The New York Times, Boston Globe, *and the* Chronicle of Higher Education. *Dan is also the organizer and coproducer of the "Chance Lectures," a CD-ROM series focusing on the uses of statistics in real life, ranging from odds making to ESP debunking. His research is currently supported by the National Science Foundation, the Department of Defense, and the Department of Justice.*

In 1995, the White House recognized Dan's research and teaching with the National Science Foundation's five-year Presidential Faculty Fellowship. In conjunction with Cinemen Production's W. Conquest and B. Drake, he is now in the process of making a National Science Foundation-funded documentary on the process and beauty of mathematical research. (AUTHOR PHOTO BY JOE MEHLING.)

A SLICE OF PI

WELL, IT'S FINALLY HAPPENED. A number is a movie star. Sure, numbers have figured prominently in movies before, but previously, it's always been more about what a number represented than the number itself. *2001, 1984*—these were just names for years; *10* was a description of Bo Derek and *Seven* counted the number of deadly crimes that we were about to see. But in the recent movie *Pi*, the number pi is really the star.

You have to admit that as far as numbers go, pi has star quality. To begin with, it has an exotic Greek name, and when we refer to it in writing, we use a delicate and mysterious symbol, just like we do for the artist formerly known as Prince. Also, pi is already famous to people around the world, recognized since 2000 B.C. as the ratio of the circumference of a circle to its diameter. Yes, that's right, take any circle, and measure the distance around—that's the circumference—and then compare this to the diameter—which is the distance across when you go through the center. What you'll find is that you need a little more than three diameters in order to get the circumference—and the exact number you need is pi. And this is true for every circle!

So, what exactly is pi? Well, I wish I could tell you, but like many famous movie stars, pi is temperamental. You see, pi is an *irrational* number. This means that the decimal expansion of pi is full of surprises. If pi were *rational*, or in other words, a fraction, we would either get an expansion that stopped somewhere, like 3.14, or one that eventually repeated, like 3.141414. But instead, the list of digits that we get seems almost whimsical. There is no telling what will come next! *That's* irrational for you.

So, mysterious and unpredictable, but as common as a circle, the number pi teases us—it's easy to find, but hard to know. Pi is celebrity material—ready-made for the movies.

In the movie *Pi*, our newest numerical star plays the object of devotion of one Max Cohen, a young mathematical genius and loner, who is obsessed with uncovering the secret of the decimal expansion of pi. Max lives his life based on three assumptions: One, that mathematics is the language of nature; two, that everything can be represented by numbers; and three, that the numbers that represent nature must have a pattern. From this Max believes that pi *must* have a simple pattern or description. Max's research eventually pays off and he discovers a two-hundred-sixteen-digit number that encodes the secret of not only pi, but also the behavior of the stock market, and, for a strange cult of ultraorthodox Jews, a path to knowing God. The film moves between Max's pursuit of the code and various people's pursuit of Max.

As a mathematician, there were many things I liked about the movie: the idea, for instance, that mathematicians, like any good scientists, are looking for simple descriptions or patterns to describe seemingly complicated phenomena. There are implied ideas from *chaos theory* showing that even simple mathematical rules can generate models for very complicated-looking behavior, like the way that cigarette smoke swirls in the air, or cream mixes into coffee. Even the idea that the infinite number of digits in pi's expansion could be encoded in a finite list of numbers subtly shadows some very deep concepts from something called *complexity theory*.

Unfortunately, these ideas are often overshadowed by the portrayal of Max's obsessive nature and reclusiveness, and, in general, the usual mad scientist or crazy mathematician stereotype. Max can't help but see patterns and numbers everywhere. But, as I like to point out, it's not only scientists who see the world through the eye of their profession—I know businessmen who see everything as a deal and coaches who see everything in life as a game. It wouldn't surprise me one bit to hear that my auto mechanic views the world as a complicated but finely tuned machine, although movies about crazed mechanics seem to be in short supply.

Nevertheless, to be honest, Max's character does seem to be at least partially based on reality. Several years ago, an article in *The New Yorker* magazine profiled David and Gregory Chudnovsky, two brothers whose New York apartment was crammed with computer equipment mainly devoted to studying pi. Max's constant use of migraine medication and obsession with numbers seemed to echo articles and books on the recently deceased mathematician Paul Erdos.

In addition, the movie's juxtaposition of science and religion revives interesting debates about the psychology of discovery.

Ever since ancient Greece, man has worried that too much knowledge, or some kinds of knowledge, can be dangerous. I won't ruin *Pi*'s ending to tell you how this myth gets replayed here.

So, on the whole, I thought the movie was excellent—very thought-provoking, but most important, a startling debut for the number pi, which undoubtedly will open up Hollywood's doors to numbers everywhere! But, I wonder, who will pi be taking to the Academy Awards? The square root of two?

GETTING LOST TO BE FOUND

SEVERAL WEEKS AGO I found myself with a few other mathematicians and two dogs, wandering through the chilly and bare woods just past the Dartmouth Skiway, in the northeast corner of Lyme, in search of an old graveyard. We were looking for the "Tinkhamtown Cemetery," which one of my friends, Peter, a Hanover native, had heard about from his mother. The history of this possibly legendary graveyard is a bit sketchy. The land we were tromping around on had once been the property of one Ebeneezer Tinkham, a Revolutionary War veteran who had served in the Navy. Together with his son Cyrus, he had bought the land from Henry Holt. Cyrus later bought out his father's stake, but eventually he went mad and the land was sold off by his guardian. This area came to be known as Tinkhamtown, and, as the story goes, housed a small cemetery.

My friend Peter had decided he had to find the graveyard, so there we were, dogs and mathematicians, crunching through the leaves late one winter's afternoon. As we wandered around I tried to keep track of our location, but at some point I realized that I was lost. Visions of *The Blair Witch Project* began to dance in my head and I nervously asked Peter if he knew where we were. He responded dejectedly that yes he did, and that this was the whole problem, because as we all knew, the best way to find Tinkhamtown Cemetery was to get lost!

You see, what Peter had in mind was the story of another mathematician walking in the woods—the famous Hungarian mathematician, George Polya. As the legend goes, Polya was wandering in the woods outside Zurich and over the course of his walk, kept bumping into an acquaintance of his who was spending the day strolling with his fiancée. These frequent meetings became a real source of embarrassment for Polya, and that evening Polya decided to see if mathematics could help show why this kept happening.

Polya studied a simplified version of the problem, which is called "the drunkard's walk." Imagine that you are in New York City. It's been a long day and you go into a friendly local tavern to unwind. After a little bit too much unwinding you come out of the bar and start wandering randomly through the city. Like many big cities, New York is largely laid out on a grid, like a checkerboard, so that in your tipsy state, at each corner you have an equal chance of going east, west, north, or south. The question is—will you make it home? Polya proved that, assuming you can walk for an infinite amount of time, eventually you will come to every point in the city!

The implication is that Polya couldn't help but repeatedly run into the happy couple . . . well . . . assuming he was a bit drunk. History does not reveal if his friends believed him.

The sort of process that Polya studied is called a "random walk," and it is a particular example of something called a "stochastic process," a subject that has been applied to a wide range of topics, including the prediction of the stock market, genetics, and even music composition.

When you are reeling through the streets of New York this is the two-dimensional version of the problem, but the same problem can be posed in any number of dimensions. In the one-dimensional version you can only go north or south at each corner, and again the same thing happens—you visit all corners along the infinite street infinitely often. In the three-dimensional version it is as if at each corner you could also choose to go up or down—sort of like an infinite jungle gym. But in this case something strange happens—you are no longer guaranteed to visit every corner. The moral is simple: Don't get drunk in three dimensions!

Needless to say, we didn't find the Tinkhamtown Cemetery that day, but next time we'll remember our mathematics and do our best to lose our way. After all, it wouldn't be the first time that someone got lost while doing a math problem . . .

A GEOMETRY OF LIFE

ON MY WAY TO Boston one snowy night for dinner with some mathematician friends, I had a slight scare when I hit some ice on Route 93. I was a bit shaken up, but otherwise fine, and of course as I sat down to dinner I had to tell everyone the story. We then traded stories of our scariest experiences. Most of us related other tales of icy roads and bad drivers. But my friend Steve had a very different sort of story. He had been walking in Cambridge near Harvard University along the Charles River on a beautiful fall day, when out of nowhere a hubcap whizzed past his head, undoubtedly having fallen off one of the cars speeding along nearby Memorial Drive. In Steve's recollection it passed inches from his face and might have decapitated him.

The story is of course pretty dramatic, but what I remember just as well is Steve's comment, that it made him realize that the geometry of life and death is not a simple one.

So often we use geometry to describe experience. Somehow, we seem to view ourselves as tiny points moving through the space of all possible experiences, where our lives trace out long serpentine paths that curl 'round and 'round like the tail of a windblown kite. Lives intersect, run in circles, or move in parallel. Things take a turn for the worse or the better. We are well-rounded, rough around the edges, or even square. Ultimately, the paths that we trace out must end up looking like the result of a child's Etch-a-Sketch—and they are just as ephemeral. One quick shake, the picture disappears, and one game ends, leaving another to begin.

There are lots of different geometries that mathematicians consider, and Steve's point was that a geometry of life is not a simple one like the geometry of perfect lines, planes, and angles of the blocks of our childhood. This idealized geometry was originally invented by the ancient Egyptians and Babylonians before being more fully thought out by the Greek mathematician Euclid. Like much of early science, this Euclidean geometry is in some ways a reflection of a time when man still thought it possible to easily categorize the world. But we know that any map of possible experiences is not easily divided up like your favorite patchwork quilt into simple regions of varying degrees of safety or danger, or easily navigated to steer clear of trouble spots.

Just take a look outside your window. Even at first blush, the geometry of the world around is clearly not that of Euclid. The jagged edges that outline the trees, mountains, and clouds cannot be accurately described by simple lines and curves. Even look more closely at those children's blocks—the smooth planes soon give way to a complicated sponge-like cell structure also outside the realm of Euclidean description. Turn your lens in the other direction and similarly the galaxies and nebulae above us seem to have an infinite complexity.

Each of these physical phenomena is instead well described by something called fractal geometry, a non-Euclidean geometry invented in the 1970s by Benoit Mandelbrodt, a mathematician at IBM. The word *fractal* is derived from a Latin word meaning to create irregular fragments. Fractal geometry provides tools for measuring the degree of irregularity of an object, and in so doing ascribes a certain type of order to even the most chaotic looking thing. Conversely, fractal geometry also gives a way to create the chaos of nature, and is used in computer graphics to make realistic-looking pictures of landscapes and oceans.

The Greeks believed that Euclid's perfect shapes represented an objective truth of which we limited human beings could only perceive an imperfect shadow. But, as we discussed over dinner that night, it seemed to us that the Greeks had it backward, that truth is what is all around us. Life is fractal—more like a complicated piece of coral, full of unsuspecting cracks and crevices, regions where the shortest path between two points is not necessarily a straight line, where sometimes things that can be seen still can't be reached, where islands of safety can be pockmarked by unseen holes of danger. All described by a geometry far from Euclid, but closer to the truth.

Mary Barrosse Schwartz is a professional fund raiser, as well as a lobbyist, a writer, and a computer programmer. Currently, she directs a capital campaign to fund a new child-care center to serve low-to-moderate-income families in the Bennington County region. Her writing is driven by a passion for educational issues, and topics touching on the quality of life for children and their families.

Mary lives in East Dorset with her husband and three young children. She paints and—thanks to time spent living in rural Japan—she is a master of a style of Japanese flower arranging called sogetsu ikebana.
(AUTHOR PHOTO BY JOHN CONTE.)

THE PURPLE DOOR

MY YOUNGEST CHILD STARTED kindergarten a few weeks ago. His school had an opening-day celebration in the front courtyard where students heard the Graham Greene quote, "There is always a moment in childhood when the door opens and lets the future in."

Then, one by one, the children walked through a free-standing purple doorway made for the ceremony.

When I saw what was happening I moved around the crowd quickly so that I could snap a photo of my son, and I caught him in the lens at the moment he passed through the doorway. He walked through with his eyes fixed on the real door to the school ahead of him, and without turning back.

My eyes filled with tears. The emotion that swept over me took me by surprise. I found myself watching this simple event as a very important rite of passage of my youngest child.

He's ready and happy to go to school. His sisters have been in school since before he was born—and he's heard their exciting school stories. Now, he acts like he's been waiting for this day for all of his five years. He lays out his clothes at night and makes his own lunch so that he gets the right snack with the right flavor of juice for the next day. He is bursting with enthusiasm.

The purple door experience was probably more of a rite of passage for me. I've been home with my young kids for eleven years, working free-lance part-time. Now I stood wondering with some regret, did I work too much during this little guy's first years?

I imagine that other women must have been asking themselves the same questions that same morning. How do we balance what our kids need, with what we need as people—financially and emotionally? As the dust is settling from those first weeks of school, I take my walks, paint in silence, and write, while distracted by this question.

I am focused on what seems to be a period of endings with my youngest.

But a period of endings necessarily is accompanied by a period of beginnings . . . my son's future and my future as a person, as his mother.

Now that the dust is settling, I watch our kids adjusting to school, to new teachers, and classmates. I adjust to a new schedule that includes time for me to be an independent person. It is an exciting moment . . . I feel like I am walking through a purple door.

URBAN MYTHS AND INTERNET HEADACHES

I DO FREE-LANCE EDITORIAL WORK, and I use the Internet every day. Over the last three years, I've received many well-meaning warnings of new viruses, crime rings, and alerts on how to get rich quick.

At first the warnings were of new viruses that came as e-mail; your simple act of opening the e-mail could magically infect your computer. These warnings were alarming, and they came from friends who had a sister whose neighbor's son's girlfriend in Texas had had this happen to her.

Somehow I found a U.S. Department of Energy web site that specializes in Internet hoaxes and chain letters. The web site identified the warnings I'd been getting as hoaxes, reporting that no computer can import a virus by simply opening e-mail. Of course, they warned, never ever open an attachment to an e-mail without scanning it first with virus protection software that you periodically update to cure new viruses.

The DOE warns that the real virus, causing the loss of hundreds of hours of productivity in the workplace, and clogging e-mail boxes internationally, is the perpetuation of fake virus myths like these.

After the virus hoax emails, I received a few urgent warnings of kidney thieves in Texas, who are said to slip business travelers a mickey, then surgically remove and steal their kidneys to sell on the supposedly lucrative organ black market, leaving the traveler to awaken in a motel tub filled with ice with a phone close by and instructions to call 911. Huh? Apparently the same crack reporters who identified the Neiman Marcus cookie recipe as urban legend tried to track this story down, and have declared it to be a new Internet urban myth.

I've also received less exciting warnings that the U.S. Senate is considering allowing your long-distance telephone carrier to charge for your e-mails out of your calling area. Check out the DOE web site if you are interested in details, but rest assured that this isn't actually being considered by anyone right now.

Oh, and Newt Gingrich is not trying to get rid of the National Endowment for the Arts and National Public Radio funding this year. The fact that Newt Gingrich is no longer in office didn't stop a well-meaning friend from sending this warning to me this week. This e-mail chain letter was started by two well-meaning college students a few years ago, and caused their expulsion, but the warning goes on.

Another warning is that if someone calls and says they are from the telephone company and asks you to type in some number, they will then access long-distance telephone service that will be billed to you. Apparently this warning was issued to employees of a company that had a PBX telephone system, where this can happen. But instead of the warning stopping with the people that could be harmed, it has gone on . . . and on . . . to those who can't.

Oh, and if you continue the chain letter, Bill Gates will not give you a free trip to Disney. He just won't, even though the well-propagated chain e-mail promises.

Of course, then there are the people who sit at their computers, probably at work, thinking up spoofs on the hoaxes:

"This virus will rewrite your hard drive—not only that but it will scramble any disks that are even close to your computer. It will recalibrate your refrigerator coolness setting so all your ice cream goes melty. It will give your ex-girlfriend your new telephone number."

Just remember, if the language sounds very technical—using phrases like "the nth-complexity binary loop"—it is probably a hoax. And if the warning comes from a federal agency that doesn't deal with Internet issues—like the FCC—it's a hoax.

And don't send a warning without checking with a credible source—at least not to me.

CHILD CARE COUNTS

✑

GOVERNOR DEAN DECLARED May 12, 2000, Child Care Provider Appreciation Day in Vermont. It's an opportunity to thank the people who take care of children while their parents are at work. It's important that we thank our child-care providers, and that we keep them in mind more than one day a year. They work hard, teach and love our kids, and are often paid very little, with poor benefits.

Many working families are having a tough time finding child care in Vermont. As a result, the state is facing a child-care crisis. With seventy-five percent of Vermont mothers with children under six in the work force, private and public resources are needed.

The shortage of child care means more people are having difficulty staying in the work force. With very low unemployment throughout Vermont, large and small businesses are feeling the crunch of attracting and retaining workers. High turnover and job vacancies are bringing the issue home to businesses, large and small.

I've gone to work locally fundraising for a child-care center that's addressing the shortage by building a new facility to double the number of available slots there. The new slots are critical to the economic sustainability of the entire region, and to families that need the child care simply to earn a living.

But even if all communities have new child-care slots, working families who earn very low wages are having trouble paying for child care. There is a state subsidy, but depending on where you live in Vermont the subsidy barely covers the cost. A study prepared by Art Woolf of Northern Economic Consulting for the Child Care Fund of Vermont showed that the gap between the subsidy and the cost of care is large in some areas because the subsidy is based on state averages of child-care cost. He estimates that it would require "five million dollars in additional state spending to make child care more affordable by basing those subsidies on regional costs rather than state average costs."

The research shows that there are slots for nearly 30,000 children in licensed and home-centered day care. "This seems like a lot," he says, "but it represents only forty percent of the children under nine." With seventy-five percent of the mothers of children under six working, this is a huge problem.

Businesses are natural candidates to help to bridge the gap for employees. The Vermont Community Foundation sponsors a component fund called the Child Care Fund of Vermont, which is dedicated to "building a long-term, sustainable base of financial and moral support to strengthen and improve child care in Vermont." It publishes a handbook to help businesses find solutions to problems of child care, which is available by calling 802–863–4188.

The Child Care Fund, with *Vermont Business* magazine, also publishes annually an honor roll of the "Vermont employers who offer family friendly business programs, and who recognize the importance of high quality child care." This year's winners of the top awards are Bell Atlantic, Hemmings Motor News, and Lamoille Valley Veterinary Services.

But clearly, it is the employees and their kids who are the real winners.

A native of Providence, Rhode Island, Bill Seamans fought in the infantry during World War II. He is a veteran of the Northern France, Ardennes, and Rhineland campaigns. Following the war, he attended the Columbia Graduate School of Journalism, and from there made his way to CBS News.

Bill's ten years at CBS included time as a writer, an assignment editor, and as the executive TV news producer. In 1963, CBS News gave way to NBC, where he spent nearly thirty years producing and writing news.

Not surprisingly, Bill Seamans frequently found himself at the flash points of world events during these years, both as NBC's director of news coverage, Europe, and as Middle East bureau chief and correspondent.

(AUTHOR PHOTO BY ABC NEWS.)

LEXICON

THE IMPEACHMENT CONTROVERSY IS officially over, but it leaves behind a considerable contribution to the Beltway dialogue. So pungent is this nouveaux expression that I thought it would useful to ruminate on how many new scandal-minted words might achieve posterity in Webster's dictionary.

Monica Madness and all those investigations ending with the suffix "-gate" became part of our TV culture. So it was inevitable that the talking heads acquired an identity as unique as their discussions. We called them the "punditocracy," thereby raising the rank of pundit to a higher level of celebrity. They engaged in what were called "gabathons" and they became known as "bloviators," or "hyperverbilators," or perhaps "chatterati."

There was so much talk, talk, talk that we, the people, are said to have suffered a seizure of "mediaphobia"—more or less defensively described by *The New York Times* as "not a concern about real problems but an anxiety disorder—an increasingly irrational spiral of often unwarranted fear of the news media." This affliction was a symptom of a discomfort called "scandal fatigue," which we suffered as the Republican congressional prosecutors told us they were interpreting the Constitution by "connecting the dots," thereby elevating that simple childhood game to historical grandeur by placing it in the Congressional Record.

The Republicans repeatedly claimed that their efforts to impeach President Clinton were truly bipartisan. The somewhat skeptical Democrats agreed, sort of. They called it "unilateral bipartisanship." We got so-called White House "spin" from daily briefings. The gathering of reporters for those sessions was called a "gaggle." The news secretary du jour—Mike McCurry or Joe Lockhardt—spent much of his time denying what were called "blowback" stories. These were unconfirmed charges from unidentified sources of alleged unproven Clinton misdeeds that the responsible mainstream media refused to report. They then were planted in sensationalist British newspapers owned by Ruppert Murdoch, one of Clinton's arch-critics. These stories would then "blowback" to the States, when they were picked up and spread by more Murdoch-owned media like the *New York Post* and the Fox news network, or by Matt Drudge, the cyber gossip who also works for Murdoch.

The word "parse" zoomed to the top of the buzzword (from the word "buzz," meaning gossipy stuff) list when all Washington tried to interpret President Clinton's definition of what the true meaning of the word "is" is. If anything gave us some brief relief from mediaphobia it was, indeed, the fact that one could not use the word "is" without a smile.

One of the most prolific wordsmiths was Maureen Dowd, the rapier computer columnist of *The New York Times*, who drove her readers to the dictionary when she used the word "ithyphallic" as her favorite description for President Clinton. She called the scandal dialogue "sinuendo," and from "bimbo eruptions" she evolved the descriptive words "bimbroglio" and "bimbonic plague."

Kenneth Starr acquired the nickname "Keyhole Ken" after he produced his sex-laden report, which was the birth of a new porno-puritan literature of voyeurism. The loquacious lawyer

Alan Dershowitz dusted off some Congressional history when he called Keyhole Ken's treatment of some witnesses "sexual McCarthyism." Yet despite Starr's extreme probing of private lives, it became in some quarters very "in" to be summoned by him to testify.

Those not on Starr's hit list suffered a seizure diagnosed as "subpoena envy"—a condition enflamed by visions of the enhanced celebrity of appearing on TV talk shows and snagging one of those highly lucrative instant tell-all book contracts. It proved, as has been said, that we live in a world in which a book can be written by someone who has never read one.

With new words came new meanings. Linda Tripp gave poignancy to the adversarial expression "I've been tripped up." She also gave more feeling to the meaning of the words "friendship," "surrogate motherhood," and "let's do lunch." And adding to the new word list was the contribution of porno publisher Larry Flynt, whose outing of Congressional adulterers became known as "Flynting." It was said Fear of Flynting was one of the main reasons that our honorable legislators wrapped up the hearings as soon as possible.

Sadly, the new Beltway lexicon drove out another list of words—civility, integrity, respect, loyalty, and truth. And for some of the personalities who seized their fifteen minutes of celebrity we add the words, "fame is sometimes just another variety of infamy."

HUSSEIN

SO MANY PROFOUNDLY GENUINE, moving, and heart-touching words of praise have been spoken about him that there is hardly anything more one can say—but a week's distance from his funeral does enable a less emotional look at how King Hussein involved us all in an appreciation of his character and personality. It also gives time to recall memorable moments experienced by those who have met him.

As I watched the exceptional turnout of world leaders say their farewells, I could not help but think of what was going on at the same time in Washington. What a disheartening contrast for an American to see how the leaders of the greatest and most powerful nation in history have diminished themselves while the leader of one of the smallest of nations rose above all others as an exemplar of integrity.

King Hussein was liked and disliked by both friend and foe at one time or other, but there was one response that brought them all to his funeral in Amman last week—respect. Respect for his courage and integrity. Respect for his unique political skill. Respect for his dedication to the peace effort in the Middle East where Arab and Jew, he would remind us time and again, were both the children of Abraham.

When the king rose from his sickbed to attend the signing at the White House of the Wye agreement reached by the Palestinians and Israel, we all listened with respect. There he stood, withered and weak, his hair shorn by chemotherapy—in effect, putting his life where his words were. This small, frail, and yes, dying figure was the largest person at the signing ceremony. He had respect.

I first met King Hussein when I was sent to produce an ABC News interview at his royal palace in Amman after the 1967 Six Day War. This was among his early encounters with a foreign television news crew, and although he was an extraordinary public speaker he was not yet comfortable with the TV camera. In the ornate sitting room, he watched with extreme interest as my crew set up our camera, lighting, and sound equipment. He looked over their shoulders, looked through the lens, fiddled with the amplifier, and asked many questions because, as we now know, he was extremely interested and adept in things mechanical—including his Harley-Davidson, his helicopter, and the royal jet that he flew as a qualified pilot.

As the interview got underway, King Hussein projected his discomfort with the camera with some stiffness and uncharacteristically stilted responses. After some minutes I stopped the interview. Interrupting the king raised the eyebrows of his security men standing nearby. I asked if I could have a word, and he invited the crew to go into the next room where coffee was served. We remained alone ("alone" always means with bodyguards present) in the sitting room, and I took a deep breath and bit the proverbial producer's bullet. I apologized for the interruption and explained that he did not sound and look natural.

"What should I do?" he asked.

My advice was the usual basic producer-speak—just relax—forget the camera—just carry on a normal conversation with the interviewer.

After a few more minutes, and more pungent Arabic coffee, he suggested we resume the interview and said with a smile, "Relax—you seem a little uncomfortable. Be assured that I know the difference between criticism and the integrity of good coaching—and I appreciate your efforts."

The interview went off smoothly and comfortably and was well received back in the States because it was one of King Hussein's first commentaries after losing the West Bank and Jerusalem to Israel.

I later found out how much King Hussein did appreciate our efforts because every Christmas thereafter until cancer overwhelmed his usual activities, I received cards from him wishing me the season's greeting. They included family portraits—mostly of his children taken by the King himself, an amateur photographer of really professional ability.

I tell this personal story as an example of how King Hussein was able to reach out to ordinary people as well as the extraordinary. It is one thing to say "Thank you"—it is another to say "Thank you" and follow up with a greeting more often thereafter than really necessary. That's just one of the several reasons why King Hussein had respect.

FOREIGN LEGION

SINCE THE END OF the Cold War, we are reminded that we now are the only superpower in the world. We also hear a national dialogue arguing whether that unique position of power means we also should be the world's policeman, as we are trying to be in Yugoslavia. We are debating whether we should draw a line between our assumed moral responsibilities and our own national political, economic, and security interests. Should they be separated? Should the cream of our American youth be sent into harm's way (that's political-speak for "sent to die") for what seem like ultrasophisticated globalization ideals and objectives that ordinary people find hard to understand?

As global cops, President Clinton insists we will not send in ground troops unless there is a permissive environment, without defining the word "permissive." The political definition seems to be that we should wage war but not disturb the people back home with the sight of body bags. Meanwhile, we are shown yet again that conventional missiles and bombs can destroy enemy lives and property but not their will to resist. So how can we fulfill our role as global cops and back up our authority with deadly force without suffering casualties of our own?

Well, how about organizing an American Foreign Legion like the famous French Foreign Legion, which is one of the toughest fighting forces in the world? It is a highly trained mini-army of several brigades of paratroopers with their own artillery and tanks, which provides the military muscle to back up French diplomacy, without disturbing the French ambience with the sight of young Frenchmen coming home in coffins. The French Foreign Legion is a mercenary force whose ranks receive legal sanctuary and anonymity in return for assuming the risks of military action, going into harm's way, for their sponsors.

Like the French, an American Foreign Legion would take in volunteers of any nationality, race, or creed if they could meet the very tough physical requirements. They would enlist for five-year terms and most often, as in the French Foreign Legion, they would probably join to escape some personal, legal, or political crisis. Once he has joined, under an assumed name and identity if he wishes, the American Foreign Legionnaire would receive legal sanctuary and protection as long as he serves under the cover of the anonymity rule, which only he can break.

Because the volunteers would come from all over the world, we would have a force among whom some could speak the language wherever we might send them overseas. The French say that, having given up all his roots, the Legionnaire is absorbed into a military family bound by discipline, solidarity, and a respect for tradition. The bottom line, the French say, is that a Legionnaire is seldom an angel but never a criminal. The French Legionnaire is offered citizenship if he serves his term with honor. We could do the same for ours.

Now, with an American Foreign Legion we could wage the small flash-fire infantry wars of the world policeman without losing any of our own youth. It would be warfare without death for Americans. This would make our politicians happy because no flag-draped coffins would be coming home to their districts.

And those among the American public who want our military sent into harm's way would also be happy because they could have their war and avoid sending someone else's sons to die for some debatable geopolitical reason.

And we all could sit back and carry on life as usual and tune in to watch our war on television without that awful burden of guilt.

Tom Slayton has been editor-in-chief of Vermont Life *magazine for the past sixteen years and is past president of the International Regional Publishers Association. Prior to his association with* Vermont Life, *he was a reporter, arts writer, and editor for Vermont newspapers for twenty years. His book* Sabra Field, The Art of Place *was published in 1993. Another book,* Finding Vermont, An Informal Guide to Vermont's Places and People, *was published in 1986, and various national magazines and newspapers have published his articles. He lives in Montpelier with his wife, Elizabeth.*
(AUTHOR PHOTO BY JOHN LAZENBY.)

MATTHIESSEN

AN AURA OF GRAVE SADNESS surrounds Peter Matthiessen like a chilly mist. Matthiessen, the internationally known writer-naturalist, is reserved and quiet, and the features of his long, heavily lined face are etched with the residual melancholy of one who has watched the slow destruction of the natural world that he loves.

He smiles, but even in his smiles, a sad irony lives. "You might as well have fun as you're going down the tubes," he told a Vermont environmental organization earlier this year.

Matthiessen has good reason to be grim. In the ongoing struggle to preserve some of the world's wild places and wild creatures from human rapacity, he sees nature constantly losing.

His most recent book, *Tigers in the Snow*, is about the endangered Siberian tiger. In the course of researching that book, he came close to several radio-collared tigers and actually saw one from an airplane as she bounded in enormous leaps through two feet of fresh snow. Though a tiger-restoration program is helping to save the Siberian tiger as a species, all four of the individual tigers that Matthiessen personally followed were eventually killed by poachers.

He's also studying cranes, which, like tigers, are a so-called "umbrella species": If you save them, you save much of the rest of their ecosystem besides. But eleven of the world's fifteen great cranes are endangered, and four or five are on the brink of extinction.

What's endangering the cranes and the tigers and the wild places they depend on is people and what people all too often do—habitat destruction, water pollution, runaway development, and wars—"the same things," said Peter Matthiessen, "that are endangering humans." He chided his audience none too gently for not opposing such destruction more vigorously.

"This is the greatest country in the world," he said. "Why do we repeatedly elect third-rate people to lead us? Are we citizens or consumers?"

Toward the end of his talk, I slipped away because I had an appointment with another rare bird that I knew had been seen not two miles from where we sat. Dusk was failing earlier, and I wanted to have one more chance to see this bird: a rare Central American flycatcher with a two-foot-long tail. It had been spotted several times in a marshy pasture near Lake Champlain. As I drove back roads toward the site, I knew this was probably my last chance to see it.

I turned onto the road to the bird's haunts and saw right away that I was not alone; a couple of other cars turned also, and when I got to the pasture, a group of birders was already there. One of the cars pulled up behind me and parked as I pulled out my binoculars, and out stepped none other than Peter Matthiessen, tall and impeccably gloomy. He's an accomplished birder, and like all the rest of us, he was there hoping to see the rare flycatcher.

Dusk was gathering in earnest now and there was no fork-tailed flycatcher to be seen. But then suddenly, a woman gasped and pointed. "Over there!" Sure enough, as if on cue, the bird had materialized in a row of nearby trees. Even more amazing, the next instant it flew to center stage and parked itself on a tree branch not forty feet from where we stood. Then it sat there with that flycatcher air of supreme self-confidence, its impossibly long tail feathers dangling, as the little crowd of bird-watchers at the fence feverishly took turns at the scopes and binoculars.

When everyone had taken at least one look, the bird took off, towing its long tail through the air as its admirers jumped and shouted. "It flew over that row of trees!" someone said. "Headed for Guatemala!" said Peter Matthiessen, grinning broadly.

And for the first time that evening, the weight seemed to lift from the shoulders of the great writer and his ingrained sadness seemed to leave him, however briefly.

Encounters with the natural world will do that, I thought as I walked back to my car, the late-summer darkness falling over the pasture. The green world heals, undeniably. Which is another reason to continue the fight to save it.

CLARINET MAN

I ALWAYS HAD A soft spot in my heart for Richard Haupt, the clarinet man, and my guess is that a lot of other Vermonters did also. Richard played the clarinet—incessantly and not surpassingly well—on the Church Street Marketplace in Burlington.

He died earlier this summer in New Orleans.

Rain, shine, snow, sleet, incipient tornado, gale-force winds—nothing could keep Richard from making his appointed rounds and playing his appointed songs on Church Street. He played his clarinet all summer and he played all winter, too, bundled to the teeth, a wool hat pulled down to his eyes, but his fingers bare to the cold—so he could play.

He was not afflicted with that disease of our time, the disease of professionalism. Richard was an amateur, and he played his clarinet for the love of it.

At first, people were put off by his wandering tempos and occasional off notes. There were complaints, and the complaints had some validity; he did sometimes sound like the last clarinet in the junior high band.

But Richard persisted. He played and played and played that clarinet, and after a while people began to like to see him on Church Street. He became a fixture, first, and later a folk hero.

Burlington is a small, proud city with a long, interesting history. But it's a Yankee city: a bit uptight and repressed. Church Street Marketplace, as bright and wonderful as it is, has enough of the upscale about it to make many native Vermonters a tad nervous.

Richard and his clarinet gave downtown Burlington something it needed: He gave it some soul.

After a few years, Richard became a well-established feature of Church Street and the marketplace. If you went there in July or you went there in January, chances were pretty good you'd see the small, mousy man with a burr haircut hunched intently over his clarinet, noodling out his version of "Satin Doll," or "When the Saints Go Marching In."

Very few people knew who Richard was or where he came from. A wonderful feature story by *Burlington Free Press* writer Molly Walsh filled in some of those details.

Born in Randolph, Richard Haupt was diagnosed as developmentally disabled at an early age. He never went beyond grade school, and could only write his name with great effort.

His mother sheltered him, moving to Florida with Richard in the fifties. After his mother's death, he came back to Vermont where his sister helped him establish a life of his own.

Richard was married twice and fathered a son. He was as good a father as his circumstances and mental abilities allowed him to be, probably a better one than many. He worked for years as a dishwasher, and somewhere along the way, he learned to play clarinet by ear.

Then Church Street and the marketplace beckoned. Molly Walsh said it well in *The Burlington Free Press*: "He played in snow flurries and the cruelest summer sun," she wrote. "At Christmas, he tooted out 'Joy to the World.' On St. Patrick's Day, he played 'Danny Boy.' Year-round, Haupt shuffled and swung to jazz standards like 'Satin Doll' and show tunes like 'New York, New York.'"

The clarinet man made records and played with local bands, including the famous spelled-with-a-P Phish. Like most of us humanoids, he had dreams of grandeur: rock-band stardom, riches, fame, and world travel. It was pursuing those dreams that he went to New Orleans this spring. He died there, after a heart attack, in July. He was sixty years old.

Richard was a statistic in New Orleans, as he probably was a statistic, or less, to the rich and powerful in Vermont. But after his death, Church Street remembered him. There was a parade of about one hundred of the Church Street regulars, a short memorial, and someone scrawled on the sidewalk: "We love you, Richard."

There's something in all of us that instinctively likes a little guy, waging a courageous fight against what seem like hopeless odds. But more than that, we love the little guy who does that—and dances while he does it.

The creative urge is universal. Richard Haupt was everyman, playing the best he could, lightening all our loads while lightening his own.

I'll miss him. And I really love Vermont for missing him, too.

PEACHAM TRAGEDY

WE LIKE TO THINK of Vermont as a place where people care about their neighbors and help one another. We may even at times get to feeling a bit smug about this good place we live.

Well, here is a cautionary tale to help ward that smugness away. It is a fit story for a long winter since it happened one winter many years ago, and its subject is winter—the winter that can freeze all compassion out of a human heart.

The story is "The Peacham Tragedy," and if it chills you to your bones and shatters a few warm stereotypes about Vermont in the process, so be it. It's a story that today's Vermonters need to hear and remember.

There were homeless people 150 years ago, as there are now, but there were no shelters to house them nor meals programs to feed them. Some towns had poor houses, but to have to go there was a terrible disgrace. Mostly, the homeless lived with their relatives, moving from home to home as their welcome wore out or circumstances directed.

One such person was seventy-four-year-old Esther Emmons, who had been living with her son, but had to move on. She decided to go to the home of her sister in Peacham, more than twenty miles away. How would this seventy-four-year-old woman get to Peacham? She was poor, so she would walk. Mary, her thirty-five-year-old daughter, and Willie, her eight-year-old grandson, also poor, also homeless, would walk with her.

The day of their long journey was cold and the weather quickly worsened. Clouds darkened the sky and the wind began to blow. Barely halfway to Peacham, Mrs. Emmons decided that they had best stop. There were few houses on the long, lonely road through Peacham Woods. They asked for shelter at the home of a Mr. Bean, but he turned them away.

Cold, dispirited, they had no choice but to continue walking. But they were getting more and more tired. And now it began to snow, at first light flakes, then heavy crystals, finally a hard, gray blizzard, whipped against them by the punishing wind. But they kept pushing forward because they knew they must reach shelter.

A man driving a light one-horse sleigh overtook them and offered the old lady a ride. His exhausted horse could pull her, but not all three of them. Esther Emmons grimly declined. She could not leave her daughter and grandson alone. The sleigh left them and they continued walking.

Just as it was getting dark, the trio emerged from the deep woods into open country and came to the farm of a man named Stewart. The farmer was outside, watering his cattle as they approached and begged him for a night's stay. But Stewart turned them down, gruffly saying he was taking no one in that night.

This left the elderly Mrs. Emmons and her two charges in desperate straits. Darkness had enveloped them and it was hard to see the road. The storm rose in fury, and they were chilled through, perhaps already frostbitten, surely shivering with hypothermia and reaching the limit of their endurance. Worst of all, despair filled their souls. Would no one help them?

The Farrows, a kindly family, lived just a mile away, but Mrs. Emmons was now totally spent. As the three wanderers stumbled down the road, she fell in the knee-deep snow again and again. Finally, breathing heavily, she fell and did not rise.

Willie and Mary pushed on, but lost their way and wandered into a field. Willie apparently saw a light from the Farrows' farmhouse window. He crawled toward it, but the light went out and he, confused, turned back to the storm to die.

The bodies of all three—Esther, Mary, and little Willie—were found the next day, where they had frozen to death. The Farrows had heard the cries of Mary and Willie, but had thought, mistakenly, that the screams came from their own demented daughter confined in an upstairs bedroom.

When Peacham learned of the tragedy, its citizens recoiled in horror. In church, the Rev. P. B. Fisk declared that neither the cold nor the storm was to blame for the tragedy.

The real blame belongs to the hard-hearted who cast out the poor, the preacher declared. "Those who thrust them out bear the guilt."

And in Peacham it is still said that guilt followed farmer Stewart to his grave. Legend says that he died shivering and cold, even though it was July.

The real chill of winter, it seems, is in the human heart. That was true in 1869, and it is true today. As we modern Vermonters consider the problems of poverty and the homeless, we would do well to remember Rev. Fisk's words:

"Those who thrust (the poor) out bear the guilt."

[Author's note: I am indebted in my retelling of "The Peacham Tragedy" to Louis Lamoreaux's version, published some years ago by *Yankee* magazine.]

A freelance writer living in Rutland, Vermont, Libby Sternberg has been involved in political and education advocacy for nearly ten years. In addition to her regular political and social commentary for Vermont Public Radio, Libby has written for the Center for Education Reform's "Parent Power" newsletter, as well as other publications on health care and education. Her work has appeared in The Weekly Standard, Insight, The Indianapolis Star, The Baltimore Sun, *and* The Christian Science Monitor.

Libby is the coauthor of The Epidemiology of Quality *(Aspen, 1995), a book on health care, and she is a member of the Romance Writers of America. A semifinalist in the Writers Connection Screenplay and Fiction contest in 1995, she recently received an award for her "Outstanding Contributions to Liberty" from a public interest law firm, the Institute for Justice.*

In addition to teaching public relations at the College of St. Joseph, Libby Sternberg has three children. She is coeditor of a weekly newsletter focusing on Vermont politics. (AUTHOR PHOTO BY CHURCH FAMILY ALBUMS, NORTH CAROLINA.)

THANK GOD FOR THE ATOM BOMB?

THIS WEEK MARKS THE fifty-fifth anniversary of the days in which the United States "sowed the whirlwind." Fifty-five years ago, the United States dropped the first atom bombs on Hiroshima and Nagasaki. Ever since then, there has been a debate about whether these bombings were necessary. Even today, picking up a copy of *Compton's Encyclopedia*, one can find this entry under a history of bombs: "Many people have declared that . . . the bombings hastened Japan's surrender, thus saving countless lives on both sides. Others have argued that it was not necessary to kill so many people . . . with such horrifying weapons and the bombings did not significantly shorten the war."

It's not unusual to see editorials and commentaries around this time of year that take the latter point of view in hand-wringing, guilt-ridden tones of high moral dudgeon. Personally, I don't think this is a bad thing. Dropping atom bombs, after all, is worth a little hand-wringing.

The man who made the ultimate decision to drop the bombs did his own fair share of hand-wringing. "We have discovered the most terrible bomb in the history of the world," President Harry Truman wrote in his diary on Wednesday July 25.

Despite his reservations about the bomb's potential, Truman's primary concern as commander-in-chief was saving American lives. Truman was the first president in modern history to have actually served among ground troops. He understood the "god-awful" work of infantry and artillery. In other words, he knew firsthand what an invasion of Japan would be like and the horrible costs it would incur.

There is ample evidence that an invasion of Japan would have cost many more lives than the bombings themselves did. And there is equally strong evidence that the Japanese had no intention of surrendering, despite the fact that they knew they were losing. In fact, even after Nagasaki was bombed, a war council in Japan ended in a deadlock as that country's supreme commanders debated whether to "lure" the Americans ashore to attack. "Would it not be wondrous for this whole nation to be destroyed like a beautiful flower?" asked General Anami, Japan's war minister at the time. After the Emperor announced the country's surrender, the officers of one Japanese infantry battalion killed themselves in the following numbers: one major, three captains, ten first lieutenants, and twelve second lieutenants. They could not face the humiliation of surrender.

This statistic is found in a provocative essay by Paul Fussell, entitled "Thank God for the Atom Bomb." Fussell was one of those ground troops who would have been sent into Japan during an invasion. After the war, he eventually taught at the University of Pennsylvania, the University of Connecticut, Heidelberg University, and at Rutgers. But he points out that the vast majority of those who experienced ground combat in the war were "not elaborately educated people." Therefore, when the John Kenneth Galbraiths of the world start to argue eloquently why the lives of ground troops should have been sacrificed in an invasion instead of dropping the bombs, these people are "silent." "Few of those destined to be blown to pieces if the main Japanese islands had been invaded went on to become our most effective men of letters or impressive ethical theorists," wrote Fussell. He's right. They went on to lead quiet lives raising families, and working hard. I know. My dad was one of them, in a ship in the Pacific headed for Japan when the bombs were dropped. His life, among many, was spared by Truman's decision.

Over a half century later, it's easy to pass judgment on those who had to make the horrible decisions of August 1945. This annual ritual of conscience-examining is a good thing. But it shouldn't drift into facile conclusions unrelated to the reality of the time.

Reality is what Truman dealt with to the best of his ability. When he was a judge in Jackson County, Missouri, Truman allowed a crooked contractor to steal $10,000 in order to forestall the theft of ten times that amount, says Truman's biographer David McCullough. Was it right to permit an evil to prevent a greater evil? "You judge it, I can't," Truman wrote at the time. My thoughts exactly on this sad anniversary.

SILENCE IS NOT GOLDEN

RECENTLY, SISTER HELEN PREJEAN was in Vermont to speak at a college commencement. Sister Helen is the Catholic nun who shot to fame when Susan Sarandon portrayed her in the film *Dead Man Walking*, the story of the nun's ministry to death row inmates.

"Thank God in Vermont . . . you don't have the death penalty," said Sister Helen at the commencement. "You're a life people. Don't let Vermont get on that death track."

In one sense of the word, however, Vermont really isn't a "life" state. Vermont ranks as one of the top states in the country for lack of restrictions on abortions. Many people, I am sure, consider this a good thing. But I suspect that a great many more just don't have the opportunity to really explore the abortion issue and how it relates to public policy. It's such a flash point that most people like to avoid discussing it altogether—especially at campaign time. Candidates who favor regulating and restricting abortions are often the subject of media stories on how their "pro-life" position will affect the outcome of the race. Little is printed or broadcast, however, exploring the nuances of the issue itself.

Before I go any further, I beg you to listen closely to the following qualifier. If you must use labels, then consider me *pro-choice*. As far as early-trimester abortions go, I support them remaining safe and legal. But I don't oppose other reasonable restrictions and regulations on abortion.

To abortion rights absolutists, then, I might be labeled pro-life. This ambiguity illustrates, however, what I think is a healthy shift in abortion discussion. People rarely fall into staunch pro-life or pro-choice camps any more. More often, they straddle the middle ground as I do, troubled by a society that they think might be taking life a little too cavalierly but equally concerned that reasonable freedoms remain protected.

Regardless of whether you are pro-life, pro-choice, or in the middle—and even regardless of whether Vermont is a pro-life or a pro-choice state—we shouldn't be afraid to explore this topic. This fearlessness, by the way, should also include a vigorous condemnation of those who use violence against abortion providers.

Nationally, abortion has come front and center in the past few years as Congress took up restrictions on partial birth abortion in addition to some parental notification laws. Major newspapers, most notably *The New York Times*, became excellent debating forums where the topic was explored eloquently and expertly on the op ed pages. The *Times*, for example, printed an opinion piece several years ago by former surgeon general C. Everett Koop, in which he explained why he supports banning partial birth abortion, the procedure labeled infanticide by some. The American Medical Association, by the way, also supports a ban on this procedure. This fact, I have found, is not well known in Vermont where we don't discuss the issue much at all. Another *Times* article, written by an abortion provider and staunch pro-choice advocate, spoke of why parental notification laws are necessary and deserving of passage.

Recently, some Vermont legislators heard testimony on the need for parental notification laws and regulation of abortion facilities. You might not be aware of the fact that in Vermont a minor is required to get parental consent, not for abortions, but for tattooing. Seems strange, doesn't it? As one mother testified to the legislature after her daughter told the story of her own lonely abortion: "The one time in my life that I was needed most by my daughter, the state of Vermont has taken that right away from me."

Whether you agree or disagree with that mother, we should be talking about it. We shouldn't assume the conversation ended with *Roe v. Wade* and that, through that ruling, we have been absolved forever of having to think about abortion policy. Silence in this case is not golden.

To be sure, discussing abortion policy means opening up a Pandora's box full of complex questions with no easy answers. Questions like—When does life begin? Does protecting life ever become a more important public policy than protecting liberty or the pursuit of happiness? As responsible citizens, we should embrace such a search for truth and fairness. Those who would prefer not to openly debate this issue need to confront the reason why— let's hope it's not because they're afraid of the answers we'll find when we finally start asking the questions.

NO EXCUSES!

ACCORDING TO 1998 National Assessment of Education Progress (NAEP) scores, fifty-eight percent of our country's low-income fourth graders cannot read. According to *Education Week* magazine, sixty-seven percent of low-income inner-city eighth graders cannot meet basic math standards for their grade level.

It doesn't have to be this way. At a recent Washington conference entitled "No Excuses," principals from high-poverty, high-performing schools shared their successful strategies with approximately 300 attendees from across the country.

Here is a look at the themes that developed during the day:

Traditionalist strategies work: So-called "progressive education" techniques hurt low-income children, said Nancy Ichinaga, principal of the Bennett-Kew Elementary school in Inglewood, California. Seventy-eight percent of Ichinaga's students are classified as low income, yet her school has been one of the highest performers in Los Angeles County for twenty years after she dumped progressive methods espoused by her predecessor.

Other principals spoke of how they use homogeneous grouping, E. D. Hirsch's Core Knowledge curriculum, direct instruction techniques, or simple college-preparatory approaches for all kids.

Constant assessment is essential: High-performing school principals use assessment "not as an autopsy but as a physical." They are constantly monitoring how they are performing. "You teach, you assess, you teach, you assess," said James Coady, principal of Morse Elementary of Cambridge, Massachusetts.

Flexibility helps: Principals who succeed in achieving results are "risk-takers," said Gregory Hodge, principal of the Frederick Douglass Academy in central Harlem. Hodge, and each principal at the conference, had his or her own tale to tell of how they used creativity and ingenuity to get around the education bureaucracy and even the constricting red tape of union contracts.

Rewarding good teachers makes sense: Teachers at Healthy Start Academy in Durham, North Carolina, receive a "superior health insurance and retirement program." Teachers at Michael Feinberg's KIPP Academy in Houston, Texas, are paid fifteen to twenty percent more than teachers elsewhere in the state. But Feinberg worries that his talented friends eschew teaching as a career because of its lack of "upward mobility." Knowing they would be rewarded for superior work, instead of just tenured, would be a major drawing card.

The buck stops with the teacher: A "culture of success" pervades these schools. No finger pointing at too much television, too little family time, too much junk food, too little parental involvement, or too much violence on the streets.

"After all the finger pointing," said KIPP Academy's Michael Feinberg, "I started pointing the finger at myself, the teacher."

Competition is good: While each of the principals was a strong advocate of public schools, they also recognized the value of competitive pressures and incentives. For the most part, in fact, their schools were beneficiaries of choice systems.

An inspiring overarching theme, however, permeated each presentation. Low-income, minority children are just as capable of achieving high academic standards as their more advantaged peers. Anyone who makes excuses for their failure doesn't really see them as equals.

Thus far, Jeff Wennberg's career in public service has been a study in thoroughness. He began by serving a four-year stint on the Rutland City School Board and was elected board president in 1981 and 1982. In 1983 Jeff joined then-Congressman Jim Jeffords's Vermont staff as Jeffords's southern Vermont office manager—only leaving the position in 1985 to become Rutland City's planning coordinator. By March of 1987, Jeff Wennberg had become the youngest mayor in Rutland's history. He remains the only person ever elected to six terms as mayor.

In 1991 Mayor Wennberg was appointed to the Energy, Environment, and Natural Resources steering committee of the National League of Cities. He was appointed vice-chair of the committee in 1992 and 1993, and chair in 1994. Since leaving office, Jeff has served as interim municipal manager for the Town and Village of Ludlow and is currently the manager of the Rutland County Solid Waste District.

Educational issues remain extremely important to Jeff. A cofounder of Vermonters for Educational Choice, he is on the Board of Directors of Vermont Student Opportunity Scholarships Foundation. Jeff and his wife, Nancy Bevins Wennberg, have two children, Jillian and Ethan. (AUTHOR PHOTO BY GARY BOUCHARD.)

THE NEW COUNTERCULTURE

"ANSWER ME THIS," the gray-haired man demanded. He spoke with such intensity his words were a verbal index finger shoved sharply into my chest. "Why can't Johnny tell right from wrong?"

I knew this man. He had dedicated his life to the least powerful, the disabled and imprisoned. And although he was now retired, his passion for their plight was clearly undiminished.

But if his tone left any doubt, his unflinching gaze made it clear that this was not a rhetorical question. He wanted my answer.

Now. Never mind that he stumbled upon me at the town transfer station, or that cardboard en route to recycling was spilling from his trunk, or that it had been well over a year since I held public office: "Why can't Johnny tell right from wrong?"

"I don't really know, but perhaps it's because mom and dad don't teach him anymore." I knew it was lame but I had to say something.

He shook his head in disgust. "It's a hell of a lot bigger than that," he muttered. "It's no-fault divorces because mommy got bored or daddy got restless and who gives a bleep about the kid. It's little girls growing up with their children, with the father gone before the kid is born. It's healthy, bright nineteen-year-old boys who ought to be out chasing girls, instead landing in jail for the second or third time because they don't know anything else. It's the whole bleeped culture, that's what it is."

The following evening I was an invited guest at a meeting sponsored by a number of evangelical and a few mainstream Christian churches. The name on the program was "Courageous Christianity," and it occurred to me that in secular, liberal Vermont, it took more than a little courage just to show up at this politically incorrect men's-only event. Nonetheless, several hundred men of all ages filled the room.

Two days later, a friend questioned me about the event. "Was it mostly a bunch of right-wingers?" she asked. No, I said, there was zero political content to the meeting; and no, I said, civil unions were not even mentioned. It was one group of guys desperately looking for answers in a society that won't even ask the questions, and another group of guys who believe they have found the answer in Christ. "Oh," she said.

My parents grew up in the Depression and came of age during the brutality of the Second World War. The culture of prosperity and complacent suburban conformism they created was the antithesis of the world they had known.

When we came of age, the children of the fifties declared war on our parent's world, calling our nonconformist, self-indulgent alternative the "counterculture." Looking back, it's clear that today, the counterculture's moral relativism and individualistic values rule.

The counterculture became the culture. And it is ironic that we who came to power questioning all authority have no qualms about exercising it ourselves.

And just as my parents feared their children's rejection of the ordered world they created for us, those who have grown powerful and comfortable within our current culture fear the emergence of a new counterculture.

Two generations ago, advocates of equal rights or the environment were labeled communists or radicals. Today, the advocates of direct democracy or school choice for the poor are labeled bigots or anti-American.

When spray-paint-wielding vandals deface a "Take Back Vermont" sign to read "Take Back Your Hate," are they attacking intolerance or demonstrating it? I guess it all depends on which side of the cultural divide you sit.

GILLYISMS

I SUBSCRIBE TO THE pendulum theory of elections. The theory is based upon the same principle television networks use to predict the life expectancy of a new series. That is, no matter how much we like a fresh new program at first, in about six years we'll tire of it and toss it away. And it doesn't seem to matter whether the program ages like wine or milk; once it's old, we prefer whatever is new.

This same principle applies to the selection of the President. Once someone has been in office for six or more years, we tend to replace him with his opposite.

Fans and adversaries of Bill Clinton and George W. Bush agree that these men define the extremes of the "glibness" scale. Even before the Lewinsky scandal, an inside-the-Beltway cottage industry sprang up to "parse" Clinton's every utterance. He was so facile with the language, layered meanings of ordinary words had to be peeled away to discover where he had installed the escape hatch on what seemed to be a straightforward statement. Ronald Reagan was called the great communicator, but when it came to communicating something without ever actually saying it, Bill Clinton owned the patent.

George W. Bush, on the other hand, sometimes speaks as though English were his second language. It's not unreasonable to wonder whether someone who periodically stumbles over his words may also stumble while charting the course of the nation. I am pleased to report from personal experience that this is not necessarily the case.

One of my predecessors in the Rutland mayor's office mangled so many metaphors, his name has been incorporated into a colloquial word for malapropisms. Around Rutland we call them "gillyisms," in honor of four-term mayor and Vermont state senator Gilbert G. Godnick.

For example, on one occasion a pair of entrepreneurs were seeking a property tax break for their modest manufacturing plant. Gilly supported the proposal. "We got to give these guys a chance to get their feet off the ground," he said. Gilly spoke in a somewhat nasal baritone so totally different from my voice it would be difficult to prove, on the basis of our utterances alone, that we belong to the same species. He also used a street dialect so like New York that everyone was astonished to learn that Gilly Godnick was a native Rutlander.

On another occasion, he admonished the board of aldermen for moving too quickly on a proposal, saying, "Those guys is putting the horse before the cart." On yet another occasion he urged the board to hurry up with the words, "It's time to get this boat on the road."

I personally witnessed Mayor Godnick's speech at the ground breaking of a public works project, funded by the Economic Development Administration, where he said, "And I want to thank Mr. Neil Cannon of the EDA for helping us with the mountainous paperwork, and for making this supposed reality a dream."

When Jack Daley challenged Gilly for his fourth term, Jack had a lead of about 130 votes before counting the absentee ballots. However, when all the votes were in, Godnick won reelection by a thirty-vote margin. When asked by a radio reporter to what he attributed his victory, Godnick said, "Well, in the final analysis, when the people of Rutland stepped behind the iron curtain it was the sick voters that put me over the hill."

That mixed-metaphoric triple play was so remarkable, this quote led the radio newscast for three days following the election.

Mayor Godnick may not have been a great communicator, but Rutlanders always knew where he stood. He was very successful in business, popular in public office, and thirty years later is remembered as an outstanding mayor. He always seemed to enjoy the humor in his own tangled language.

President-elect Bush does not have his predecessor's command of the language, but if he governs with integrity, wisdom, and compassion, America will be well served. And maybe, occasionally amused.

CAMPAIGN 2000 PARALLELS WITH 1980

THIS YEAR'S PRESIDENTIAL CAMPAIGN has a familiar ring to it.

Thomas Friedman, the syndicated columnist for *The New York Times*, recently referred to the contest between Texas Governor George W. Bush and Vice-President Al Gore as "a choice between a man with no brain and a man with no spine."

The complaints about Bush surfaced during his primary contests with Arizona Senator John McCain.

Pundits questioned Bush's politics and intellect: "Bush is too conservative; Republicans have to nominate someone who will appeal to independents and 'Reagan Democrats' to have a chance to win in November."

"Democrats are scared to death that Republicans will nominate McCain; Bush is seen as a much easier opponent."

"George W. Bush has neither the foreign policy experience nor the intellect to handle the job."

"Apart from two terms as governor, Bush's experience is in owning a baseball team; what could be more frivolous?"

If you were paying attention to presidential politics a generation ago, you might be getting an eerie sense of déjà vu right about now.

Back in 1980, the Republican nominee would face an unpopular incumbent—Jimmy Carter—who had to fend off a challenge from Massachusetts Senator Ted Kennedy just to secure his own renomination.

The Republican race quickly boiled down to a contest between three candidates; Ronald Reagan, the conservative actor who had been elected and reelected Governor of California but had held no other elective office; moderate George Bush, a former ambassador, CIA director, and congressman who had a most remarkable government service resume, but little electoral experience; and John B. Anderson, liberal congressman from the sixteenth district of Illinois with twenty years of experience in Congress. The 1980 Anderson phenomenon was almost identical to this year's McCain movement, right down to his popularity among Vermonters.

When the nomination went to Reagan, the press howled that the once-proud GOP had been hijacked by right-wing extremists, and that a repeat of the Goldwater debacle of 1964 was sure to ensue. Democrats salivated at the opportunity to run against a cowboy actor (what could be more frivolous?) who had no clue about foreign policy, was not all that bright, and was possibly even dangerous.

Reagan selected Bush for VP, and went on to crush President Carter, fifty-one to forty-one percent in the popular vote, and by a ten-to-one margin in the electoral college. The term "Reagan Democrat" is a powerful reminder of how wrong the press were.

Like the Carter people two decades before them, the Gore people can't seem to figure out why so many independents appear to prefer the man with no brain. They know that there is a "likeability gap," which thus far has resisted every effort to reengineer Al Gore. But Carter was embroiled in a foreign policy morass with an economy in free fall. Given the current state of the nation, why does Bush lead?

Back in the early '90s, I got an insight into Reagan's popularity from an inside-the-Beltway Washington lobbyist. She had met Presidents and worked shoulder to shoulder with congressional leaders for a quarter of a century. I asked her, of all the presidents she had known, whom did she admire the most? Without hesitation she shot back, "Ronald Reagan." Given that inside-the-Beltway types were never fond of Reagan, I almost had to pick myself up off the floor. "Why?" I asked, unable to hide my amazement. "Because Ronald Reagan was the only one who didn't have to be President to define who he was. He was Ronald Reagan, the Presidency was a job."

Despite his parentage, George W. Bush appears to view the presidency as an opportunity, not a career goal. Gore wants it so badly one can imagine him positively vaporizing from the disappointment were he to lose.

Perhaps Bush's early advantage stems not from the public's distrust of intellect, but of ambition.

Afterword

We faced an almost impossible task in putting this collection together: condensing the impressive output of VPR's Commentary Series into a single, portable paperback volume. As Betty Smith's introduction makes clear, the series has benefited from the talents of many writers over the years, and many of those writers wrote many, many essays. We decided, finally, to limit this collection to the work of commentators heard regularly over Vermont Public Radio in the years 2000 and 2001; members of that group of regulars—some old hands and some relative newcomers—were free to select from their own overall body of work, some of it stretching all the way back to the series's beginning. Hence the subtitle, *Best of the Vermont Public Radio Commentaries*. In no way do we mean to undervalue the fine work of commentators who left the series prior to the year 2000, or those broadcasting occasionally during it. This is necessarily a small volume, but had we the space we would have liked to include most everything by most everybody. Variations from the actual air texts are few.

And we'd like to close with profound thanks to Mark Vogelzang and the exceptional people at VPR Colchester; Betty Smith and those at VPR Norwich; and the engineers who have contrived over the years to make so many novice commentators sound so altogether professional—Chris Albertine, Bob Merrill, Sam Sanders, and Brendon Walsh.

P.B.
J.C.

AGMV Marquis

MEMBER OF SCABRINI MEDIA

Quebec, Canada
2002